UAPs and the Afterlife

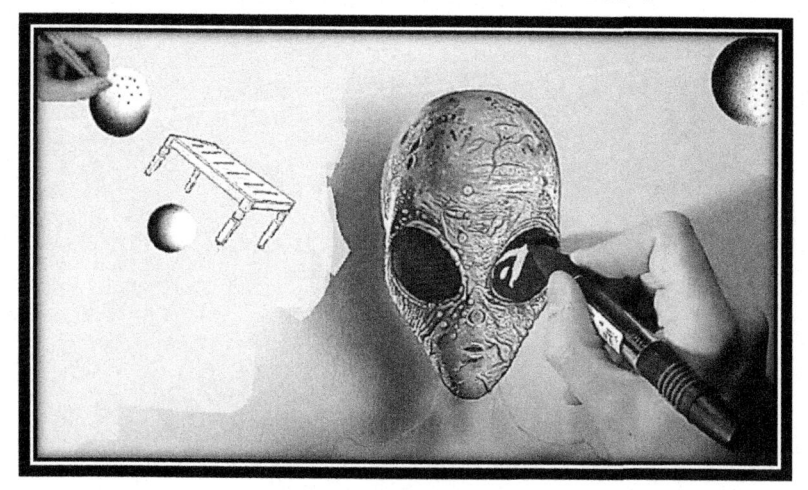

How New Disclosures Support Centuries
of Psychic and Spiritual Research

Christopher Noël

Title page illustrations: Marcello Barenghi and Ms. Cooper's Art Class

The rational study of reported cases of UFOs is currently at an impasse. This situation has as much to do with the incomplete state of our models of physical reality as it does with the complexity of the data.
—Jacques Vallée

We're part of a symbiotic relationship with something which disguises itself as an extraterrestrial invasion.
—Terence McKenna

The two central questions are: What happens to us after we die? and Are we alone in the universe? I'm increasingly led to the view that the two are linked.
—Ross Coulthart

Also by the author

There Is No Veil: At Play in the Vast Here and Now

Sasquatch and Autism: Twelve Parallels

Next of Kin Next Door: How to Find Sasquatch a Stone's Throw Away

Mindspeak: Tapping into Sasquatch and Science

Our Life with Bigfoot: Knowing Our Next of Kin at Habituation Sites

A Field Guide to Sasquatch Structures: The 50 Most Common Types in North American Forests

The Girl Who Spoke with Giants (novel)

Maggie and Fever: A Sasquatch Story (children's book)

Emergency Preparedness (stories)

In the Unlikely Event of a Water Landing: A Geography of Grief (memoir)

Hazard and the Five Delights (novel)

The Purpose of this Book

I could just as well have titled it *UAPs and Consciousness* because the afterlife *is* consciousness.

So that you can know if this book is for you, I want to lay my cards on the table up front. I'm persuaded that consciousness transcends the brain; that our individual consciousness (aka psyche: spirit) is part of a fundamental consciousness field; that with bodily death comes the return of our consciousness (still individualized) to our Source/Home; that the spirits of the departed are not actually "departed" but still exist in the same place that we do, just at a higher vibrational frequency; that these spirits can occasionally lower their frequency in order to revisit us, communicating through authentic mediums and even affecting the physical world; that an array of psychic/spiritual phenomena—e.g., telepathy, remote viewing, and psychokinesis—can be understood within this context; that the UAP enigma is located, with us, in the same fundamental consciousness field; and that these visitors are intimately akin to us, not in fact "aliens" who evolved independently, elsewhere in the cosmos.

My aim here is not to prove any of this to you; I'm concerned with *how* such things exist, not joining the tiresome debate over *whether* they exist. I want to explore the connections and resonances between and among the above aspects of reality.

A rich trove of conclusive evidence for psychic/spiritual phenomena is readily available. If you're still agnostic on the issue of the afterlife, for instance, why not become *gnostic* by spending a couple of weeks looking deeply into the situation? I made my own best case in *There Is No Veil*, but I'll recommend just five sources—*Surviving Death: A Journalist Investigates Evidence for an Afterlife* by Leslie Kean; *Consciousness Beyond Life* by Pim van Lommel; *The Scole Experiment: Scientific Evidence for Life After Death* by Grant and Jane Solomon; *Life and Afterlife* by Michael Prescott; and the essays available on the Bigelow Institute's website that were recognized as making the strongest arguments for consciousness survival:

https://www.bigelowinstitute.org/index.php/essay-contest/
https://www.bigelowinstitute.org/index.php/contest-runners-up/

UAP disclosure will inevitably involve much more than adding to the inventory of our world an extra class of objects and characters. Instead of merely revealing *what's in our world*, disclosure will confront us with *what our world is in*. Our narrow everyday perspective languishes naïvely inside a larger reality frame whose true nature will deliver a blow, virtually overnight, far more humbling and destabilizing than the drawn-out Copernican and Darwinian revolutions combined; hence, the "ontological shock" we've been told to brace for. Even the conventional alien invasion of page and screen, a straightforward technological war for the planet, would at least leave the ground of physical reality itself unchallenged, the implications easier to cope with.

Increasingly of late, sources inside the sprawling world of the UAP cover-up have sent surprising signals about the nature of our visitors and their craft.

David Grusch's July 2023 congressional testimony, under oath, revealed that the US government has conducted, for seven decades at least, a hands-on study of nonhuman "biologics"/bodies and their breathtakingly maneuverable vehicles. The prime directive has been to figure out how they fly in a manner that defies known physics, and then to reverse-engineer them in order to produce our own functional replicas and thus gain worldwide military superiority.

Since Grusch, many have probed this question: How much progress have we actually made in deconstructing and applying UAP technology? The surprising signals have suggested that, in fact, little has been made—some core secret has continued to elude us.

In early October 2023, internationally renowned journalist Ross Coulthart received a scoop, which he alluded to on the Project Unity YouTube channel.

> I can't talk about it, but I had another major nudge late last week. And it was world-rocking…like *holy hell*. What I *can* talk about is that, if this is true, a large part of what's been frustrating our attempts to reverse-engineer this technology is the shortage of people who have the capacity to consciously engage

with it. You need a particular type of person to operate it, using your *mind*.

This conforms with many other cryptic hints and veiled statements. In short, the idea inexorably coming forward is that UAPs are enabled by a principle not reducible to any nuts-and-bolts mechanisms or electromagnetic anti-gravity system. Instead, consciousness itself is the missing ingredient, the prime mover.

Very compelling as far as it goes. What I haven't heard, though, is any cogent explanation of what consciousness actually *is* such that it can allow UAPs to operate with no recognizable propulsion system, and even to appear and disappear in an instant.

No one on the UAP beat, that is, seems familiar with the long and fruitful history of psychic/spiritual research, especially since 1849. This sustained worldwide effort has developed copious evidence not only for an afterlife but also for such apparent miracles as

1. *levitation*: objects defying gravity, and
2. *apportation*: objects appearing/disappearing out of/into thin air.

Both of these bear directly, of course, upon the UAP case, and I cover them in some detail in Chapters 3 and 4.

With everyone else focusing on UAPs' alleged "advanced technology," I'm looking in the other direction—toward the forgotten advances of the past. By a century ago, the Spiritualist Movement had already established the shocking capacities of consciousness and provided the conceptual framework we sorely need today.

The prevailing materialistic paradigm of modern science severely hampers our inquiry, leaving us stumped, unable to connect the dots and tackle what Jacques Vallée calls "the truly fundamental problem—the relationship between psyche and matter."

It's this blind spot that *UAPs and the Afterlife* addresses head-on.

Christopher Noël
Montpelier, Vermont
January 1, 2024

Suggested Reading in the Foundations of Psychic/Spiritual Research

Crawford, William J., *The Reality of Psychic Phenomena*, E. P. Dutton & Co., New York: 1916.

Crawford, William J., W. J. *Hints and Observations for those Investigating the Phenomena of Spiritualism*, E. P. Dutton & Co., New York: 1918.

Crookes, William, *Researchers in the Phenomena of Spiritualism*, J. Burns, London: 1874.

Doyle, Arthur Conan, *The History of Spiritualism Vols. 1 and 2*, Cassell & Co., Ltd., London: 1926.

Gloumeline, Julie de, *D. D. Home: His Life, His Mission*, K. Paul, Trench, Trubner & co., ltd, London: 1888

Hart, Hornell and Hart, E. B., "Visions and apparitions collectively and reciprocally perceived," *Proceedings of the Society for Psychical Research* 41, 1932.

Heagerty, N. Riley, *The French Revelation: Voice to Voice Conversations with Spirits Through the Mediumship of Emily S. French*, White Crow Books, Guildford, UK: 2015.

Home, Daniel Dunglas, *Incidents in My Life*, Carleton Publishers, New York: 1863.

Lodge, Oliver, *Raymond; or Life and Death*, George H. Doran Company, New York, 1916

Myers, Frederic, *Human Personality and Its Survival of Bodily Death*, Longmans, Green, and Co., London: 1903

Richet, Charles, *Thirty Years of Psychical Research*, Macmillan, New York: 1923.

Tymn, Michael, *Resurrecting Leonora Piper: How Science Discovered the Afterlife*, White Crow Books, Guildford, UK: 2013.

Weaver, Zofia, *Other Realities? The Legacy of Franek Kluski's Mediumship*, White Crow Books, Guildford, UK: 2015.

Table of Contents

The Purpose of this Book

Prologue   "A Single Undivided Whole"..................................5

Chapter 1   How Are They?
             The Phenomenology of UAP Experiences................9
  1.1 Setting the stage
  1.2 "The five observables" and the great propulsion debate
  1.3 Shapeshifting tricksters
  1.4 Up close and personal

Chapter 2   "There Is Nothing Else...":
             The Primacy of Fields, the Illusion of Distance,..........21
  2.1 The mystery of quantum entanglement
  2.2 Action at a distance? False
  2.3 Quantum entanglement demystified
  2.4 The illusion of distance applies to time as well

Chapter 3   Why Consciousness Must also be a Field:
             Information and Psychokinesis (PK)......................27
  3.1 Beyond the five senses
  3.2 Telepathy
  3.3 Remote viewing
  3.4 Blindsight
  3.5 The field itself does the knowing
  3.6 Psychokinesis (PK) follows naturally
  3.7 Lighter than air

Chapter 4   Anti-Gravity without Technology:
             Shifting Ratios in a Fluid World............................45
  4.1 Ordinary matter and invisible (dark) matter
  4.2 A short course in mass and density
  4.3 Back to floating furniture: the buoyancy explanation
  4.4 The matter-type ratio theory (MTR)
  4.5 Confirmation from another angle
  4.6 The meaning of cold and "psychic breeze"
  4.7 Apports raise the stakes
  4.8 Playful water and a wandering pig
  4.9 The primordial synthesis

Chapter 5 The Dance of Density:
            Shrinking the "Problem Space"
            of UAPs and Spirits..73
    5.1 Seeing one level deeper
    5.2 Orbs and UAPs
    5.3 A clear MTR example from Skinwalker Ranch
    5.4 Temperature and MTR
    5.5 Clustering and the hitchhiker effect
    5.6 The kinship key
    5.7 The UAP propulsion system is consciousness
    5.8 Metamaterials as arrows to the future
    5.9 BREAKING: the P3 program

Chapter 6 UAPs and the Afterlife:
            A Shared Vibrational Neighborhood........................97
    6.1 Extraterrestrials, cryptoterrestrials, ultraterrestrials, oh my
    6.2 They're only human
    6.3 Death, density, and close encounters of the fourth kind
    6.4 "We're not from here"
    6.5 Forms of contact

Epilogue: Why Earth?..109

References...115

Appendix A: Einstein's Block Universe and the
              Illusion of Linear Time..121

Appendix B: The Experimental Evidence for
              Parapsychological Phenomena by Etzel Cardeña........127

Appendix C: How we Know Consciousness is not on the Electromagnetic
              Spectrum but Can Readily Engage with it..................149

Appendix D: Qi and Spirit..165

Appendix E: Gaining Substance: Franek Kluski's Séances.....................181

Appendix F: Signatures of Macro-PK..185

Appendix G: Dusty Old Books Ahead of their Time:
              Invisible Matter Precursors..189

Appendix H: Dr. Paul Werbos and the "Symbiotic Noosphere"...............197

Appendix I: "But How Will I Survive as Vibration?"
              The Informational Abundance of Frequencies.............199

Appendix J: Taking Ubiquity Literally:
             What if They are not "from" anywhere
             and are not even "They"?..................................203
Appendix K: The Brain as Filter..211
Appendix L: Suggested Experiments for Testing the MTR........................217

Glossary

IM   invisible matter (aka dark matter)
OM   ordinary matter
MTR the matter-type ratio theory
PK   psychokinesis

Prologue
"A Single Undivided Whole"

We tend to see this world as real, and everything else as just levels of "frequencies." These frequencies are actually realms that are just as substantial as this "physical" one.
—The Orb Project

Imagine going through a gate in a wall. Here is this great barrier. You walk through it, you turn around, and the wall and the gate have both disappeared. And you see you were always here.
—Alan Watts, "How to Play the Game"

Everything is fluid, is constantly changing, constantly coming into being and passing away.
—Heraclitus, 500 BCE

Physicists tell us that at the deepest level, everything is made up of fluidlike substances that we call quantum fields. Particles are packets or bundles of energy, each vibrating at its own unique frequency, that pop in and out of existence as a result of ceaseless fluctuations.
—Quanta Magazine, 2022

Life is fluid, dreamlike, flowing, fleeting, as we're all aware. But more than this, physical reality itself is an actual fluid in the broadest sense, as some have known for 2500 years and science has only lately rediscovered.

This substance spreads throughout the universe and gives rise to every form of matter and energy. It varies across a spectrum of densities, vibrating at higher frequencies the lower the density becomes. These gradations can be considered different fluids, but they are all part of the same continuous system; this is *quantum field theory*. "Ultimately," wrote physicist David Bohm, "the entire universe has to be understood as a single undivided whole."

In this book, I'll be exploring two subjects, our spiritual nature—also called our psychic nature, from *psyche* (soul)—and the nature of the UAP enigma in order to make out how, on several levels, the two illuminate one another and reveal their surprising kinship.

Both of these areas of human experience seem to entail an invisible world or larger reality frame from which mysterious forces, objects, and entities occasionally invade our familiar world. My goal here is to demystify, at least to some extent, these manifestations by appealing to the fundamental unity of all things. As I argued in my book *There Is No Veil*, it's a misconception for us to envision any objective separation between ordinary and psychic/spiritual reality; all that exists shares the same expansive environment, vibrating diversely, yes, but internally coherent and mutually resonating within the cosmos.

In reckoning with the perennial brain teaser posed by "trespassers" from an apparent "beyond," many take refuge in a superficially plausible concept—"Oh, I see: They must be *interdimensional*." But what does this term actually mean? Nothing specific; it's a hollow abstraction, a gesture in the dark, a placeholder signifying "?." Though we may feel we know what "another dimension" would be like—an *entirely foreign* species of existence—nobody really does. To assume that psychic/spiritual or UAP reality resides "elsewhere" is as baseless as thinking that invisible radio waves do. That's just an analogy, but consciousness frequencies, too, are always here with us; see Chapter 3.

Therefore, I won't be spending time on theoretical constructs such as the multiverse; hyperspace; traversable Lorentzian wormholes; torsion vortices; higher geometries; the quantum mirror universe; string theory with its eleven dimensions; portals to a parallel universe; etc. My focus instead will be on the interplay of two fundamental matter types—the *only* two that we know of—ordinary matter and dark matter. I think we can understand the full range of experience in terms of these two already-established basic ingredients, both ubiquitous here on Earth; see Chapter 4.

My worldview is 100% materialistic, but in an expanded sense of the term. To encompass nature in her fullest flower, we need to rehabilitate this concept and embrace a capital-M Materialism that covers *all* phenomena—including psychic/spiritual and UAP reality—

within a nondualistic frame that matches up with Arthur Conan Doyle's heretical 1919 suggestion, "Even the soul may come to be defined in terms of matter."[1]

For a discussion of immortality within a Materialistic context, see Appendix I, "But How Will I Survive as Vibration?"

Chapter 1
How Are They?
The Phenomenology of UAP Experiences

Phenomenology is the study of immediate experience, focusing on how events are encountered or perceived... the ebb and flow of lived subjectivity.
—Brown University

Mankind has always been aware that he is not alone. All the traditions carefully preserve accounts of contact with other forms of life and intelligence beyond the animal realm. Even more significantly, they claim that we are surrounded with spiritual entities that can manifest physically in ways that we do not understand.
—Jacques Vallée, *Dimensions: A Casebook of Alien Contact*

They're lying to us. It's like saying, "We're going to classify air. Or water. It doesn't exist, don't talk about it."
—Matthew Roberts, US Navy (retired)

overview

- Introducing the current state of the UAP subject with some historical background.
- The focus is on the phenomenology of the UAP experience—how they maneuver, how they appear, how their occupants behave toward us—rather than on any broad speculation as to their origins or agenda.
- This information raises fundamental questions of physics and cosmology, which will be pursued in chapters to follow.

1.1 Setting the stage

Leslie Kean and Ralph Blumenthal didn't exactly blow the lid off of United States governmental secrecy with respect to UAPs, but they did loosen it significantly with their December 2017 *New York Times* article, "Glowing Auras and 'Black Money': The Pentagon's Mysterious UFO Program." They reveal an off-the-books program and dedicated to concealing the enigma, quoting central players on the record for the first time. They interview Harold Puthoff, celebrated for his groundbreaking work in psychic phenomena. He speaks to our collective intellectual impotence in the face of UAP capabilities.

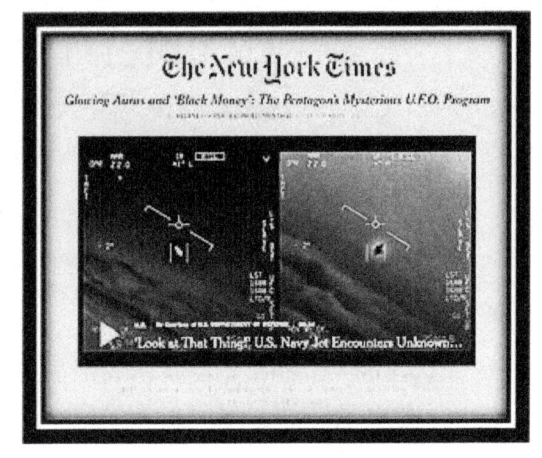

> "We're sort of in the position of what would happen if you gave Leonardo da Vinci a garage-door opener," said Puthoff, an engineer who has conducted research on extrasensory perception for the CIA. "First of all, he'd try to figure out what is this plastic stuff. He wouldn't know anything about the electromagnetic signals involved or its function."

Five and a half years later, on July 26, 2023, came the truly historic testimony, under oath, before the House Committee on Oversight and Accountability, of David Grusch, former National Reconnaissance Officer and Lead Investigator for the Pentagon's UAP Task Force. With high security clearance, Grusch had interviewed more than forty US government employees with direct knowledge of aspects of a secret, decades-long "UAP craft retrieval and reverse-engineering program" involving "nonhuman intelligence" and "nonhuman biologics"—that is, bodies.

Though many remain skeptical, and a titanic battle now rages between government forces on both sides of the disclosure question, Grusch's claims have resounded across the world. Pressure rises on fellow whistleblowers to come forward and on other nations to reveal their own intelligence on the matter.

Since you're reading this book, I'll assume you have at least a passing familiarity with the highlights of the UAP story since Roswell, 1947, including, but by no means limited to, the Lubbock lights, 1951; the Rendlesham Forest landing, 1980; the Belgium Wave, 1989-90; the Ariel School landing, Zimbabwe, 1994; the lethal interactions in Varginha, Brazil, 1996; the mass witnessing of the Phoenix Lights, 1997; and the most thoroughly documented case to date, that of the USS Nimitz off the coast of Southern California, 2004. Voluminous information on these and scores of other such modern-day visitations is available online. I recommend especially the documentaries "Ariel Phenomenon" by Randall Nickerson; "Moment of Contact" by James Fox; and "The Phenomenon," also by James Fox.

You may not be aware, however, that the saga stretches back thousands of years. The Book of Ezekiel contains what many interpret as the first recorded UAP encounter.

> 1 When I was thirty years of age, I was living with the exiles on the Kebar River. On the fifth day of the fourth month, the sky opened up and I saw visions of God.
>
> 4-9 I looked: I saw an immense dust storm come from the north, an immense cloud with lightning flashing from it, a huge ball of fire glowing like bronze. Within the fire were what looked like four creatures vibrant with life.
>
> 15-16 As I watched the four creatures, I saw something that looked like a wheel on the ground beside each of the four-faced creatures. This is what the wheels looked like: They were identical wheels, sparkling like diamonds in the sun. It looked like they were wheels within wheels.
>
> 22 Over the heads of the living creatures was something like a dome, shimmering like a sky full of cut glass, vaulted over their heads.

The historian Plutarch documents that, in the year 74 BCE, Roman general Lucullus led his twenty-five thousand soldiers into battle.

> But presently, as they were on the point of joining battle, with no apparent change of weather, but all on a sudden, the sky burst asunder, and a huge, flame-like body was seen to fall between the two armies. In shape, it was most like a wine-jar, and in colour, like molten silver. Both sides were astonished at the sight, and separated. This marvel occurred in Phrygia, at a place called Otryae.[2]

The Madonna with Saint Giovannino, late 1400s; we can see an observer in the background, gazing up.

I could add dozens more examples of such artistic renderings from the long past; see "UFO Sightings Depicted in Ancient Paintings..." on the Bright Insight channel.

In *Dimensions: A Casebook of Alien Contact* (1988), Jacques Vallée runs through myriad historical accounts. Here's a sampling.

> Japanese records inform us that on October 27, 1180, an unusual luminous object described as an "earthenware vessel" flew from a mountain in the Kii Province. On August 3, 989, during a period of great social unrest, three round objects of unusual brilliance were observed; later they joined together. In 1361, a flying object described as being "shaped like a drum, about twenty feet in diameter" emerged from the inland sea off western Japan. On March 17, 1458, five stars appeared, circling the moon. They changed color three times and vanished suddenly.

The date was September 24, 1235, seven centuries before our time, and General Yoritsume was camping with his army. Suddenly, a curious phenomenon was observed: mysterious sources of light were seen to swing and circle in the southwest, moving in loops until the early morning. General Yoritsume ordered what we would now term a "full-scale scientific investigation," and his consultants set to work. Soon they made their report. "The whole thing is completely natural, General," they said. "It is only the wind making the stars sway."

A brief examination of legendary elements in Western Europe in the Middle Ages will show that [similar testimonials] of strange flying objects and supernatural manifestations [were] spreading there. Indeed, Pierre Boaistuau, in 1575, remarked: "The face of heaven has been so often disfigured by bearded, hairy comets, torches, flames, columns, spears, shields, dragons, duplicate moons, suns, and other similar things, that if one wanted to tell in an orderly fashion those that have happened since the birth of Jesus Christ only, and inquire about the causes of their origin, the lifetime of a single man would not be enough."[3]

Even before the rise of science and its vaunted powers of discernment, thinkers were struggling to make sense of these manifestations emerging from some larger reality frame; and yet, "the causes of their origin" is no clearer today than at the time of Ezekial. The only difference is that we tend not anymore to ascribe divine Christian purpose to them or to place them within other fundamentalist contexts either. Startling ancient visitations may well have spawned the world's great religions. "This is not," Vallée continues,

> simply a case of a few tales relating encounters between a few humans and strange creatures from the sky. This is an age-old and worldwide myth that has shaped our belief structures, our scientific expectations, and our view of ourselves. I do not use the word *myth* here to mean something that is imaginary, but on the contrary something that is true at such a deep level that it influences the very basic elements of our thoughts.[4]

It's most important for our purposes, rather than multiplying reports old and new, to zero in on the central question: *How are they?* That is, *What's it like to experience them? What is their phenomenology?* You'll notice I didn't ask *What are they?*, *Who are they?*, *Where do they come from?*, or *What do they want?* This is because I want to identify meaningful parallels between UAP-related phenomena and spiritual/psychic phenomena *as these are perceived by witnesses*. This is plenty for one book. I want to understand the ways that UAPs present themselves to us, which you might call the leading edge of the matter. Beyond it lie the more far-reaching questions of "alien" origins, identity, and ultimate purpose.

1.2 "The five observables" and the great propulsion debate

"What we call unidentified flying objects are neither objects nor flying," writes Vallée. He means they do not exhibit the recognized characteristics of material things or of aviation. "They can dematerialize, and they violate the laws of motion as we know them."

Luis Elizondo, a former US Army Counterintelligence Special Agent with inside information, enumerates these violations of known physics.

1. *Instantaneous acceleration*: Objects moving in such a manner that they are capable of maneuvering suddenly, deliberately, and sometimes in the opposite direction. In some cases, these maneuvers involve a change in direction and acceleration that is well beyond the healthy limitations of any biological system that we are aware of. The anticipated effects of these g-forces on material may even defy our current technological ability to manufacture.

2. *Hypersonic velocities without signatures*: Objects that are traveling well above supersonic speeds and yet leave no obvious signature behind. Specific signatures normally include acoustic, heat, and electromagnetic, and are traditionally recognized as a sonic boom, vapor contrails, and atmospheric ionization. Currently, even the world's most advanced military and reconnaissance aircraft produce detectable signatures.

3. *Low observability*: Objects being viewed electro-optically, electromagnetically, or through the naked eye are difficult to see or visually document. Descriptions by witnesses are often confusing, while radar signals often come back nonsensical or even jammed. Objects generally appear opaque and semi-metallic in nature, but sometimes also insubstantial or translucent.

4. *Trans-medium travel*: Objects that have the ability to travel easily in various environments and conditions seemingly without any change in performance capabilities. Our current understanding of physics requires vehicles to be designed specifically according to their application. For this reason, there are stark differences between those vehicles that orbit in space, fly in the atmosphere, and travel in water. Objects that can travel in all three mediums using the same design and without compromising performance or degrading lift remain an enigma.

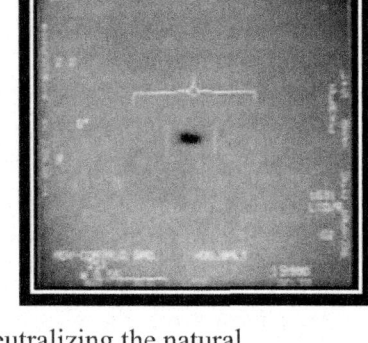

5. *Positive lift*: Objects that are apparently resisting or neutralizing the natural effects of Earth's gravity, yet without the normally associated aerodynamic means for lift and thrust. These objects have no obvious signs of propulsion (engines, propellers, exhaust plumes, etc.) or flight surfaces (wings, rudders, ailerons, fins, etc.), yet they are able to move in a very precise manner in our atmosphere.[5]

In the famous 2004 Tic-Tac incident, pilot David Fravor told CBS "60 Minutes" that

> he and Lt. Comander Alex Dietrich were training with the Nimitz Carrier Strike Group about 100 miles southwest of San Diego. At the time, advanced radar on a ship that was part of their training group, the USS Princeton, detected what operators called "multiple anomalous aerial vehicles" over the horizon, descending 80,000 feet in less than a second.

> [Fravor spotted an] object that seemed to be about the size of his Hornet jet, with no markings, no wings, and no exhaust plumes. When he tried to cut off the UAP, it accelerated so quickly that it seemed to disappear. He said it was detected on radar roughly 60 miles away less than a minute later.[6]

For the past eighty years, top aeronautics specialists, theoretical physicists, and materials scientists have thrown themselves into solving the problem of this kind of surreal maneuverability, striving to comprehend the technology involved and, perhaps, even to emulate it. In 1989, Bob Lazar, a controversial figure then and now, publicly claimed to have worked on "reverse engineering" a recovered nonhuman vehicle at a secret site called S-4, affiliated with Area 51 in southern Nevada. He shared drawings of so-called "gravity emitters," which create around the craft an autonomous gravitational field out of phase with, and immune to, the Earth's.

Lazar's trustworthiness aside, this neutralizing or offsetting of planetary gravity remains the principal goal of all such reverse engineering projects, both in the US and internationally. In order to perform as they do, UAPs would need to locally manipulate the fabric of spacetime itself, warping it into a sort of enveloping bubble and sealing itself off from the effects of both gravity and friction. The resulting "warp drive" would allow the environmentally sequestered vehicle to levitate without upward thrust; travel by modulating its private gravity and thus effectively "falling" in the desired direction (even if that would be "up" from our perspective); avoid drag effects either in the atmosphere or under water; accelerate and stop on a dime without inflicting any g-forces on its structure or occupants; and execute right-angle turns, loops, or even instant straight-line reversals with zero centrifugal issues.

1.3 Shapeshifting tricksters

Even when they're not executing "impossible" aerial and underwater maneuvers, UAPs often change form in a matter of seconds. Longtime researcher and author Linda Moulton Howe relates that

> a scientist from Sandia Labs in Albuquerque, NM, told me that he was driving parallel to a train track when he

UAPs and the Afterlife 17

saw what looked like two boxcars parked on the track. Suddenly, they rose straight up and sped off high into the sky.[7]

Such accounts abound. History is replete with them, as found in Vallée's many books. Transformations occur today, too, right before our eyes and camera lenses, forcing the inescapable conclusion that what we're dealing with, although objectively physical—sometimes witnessed by large crowds and filmed or photographed—is far trickier and more malleable than what we normally mean by "solid" matter.

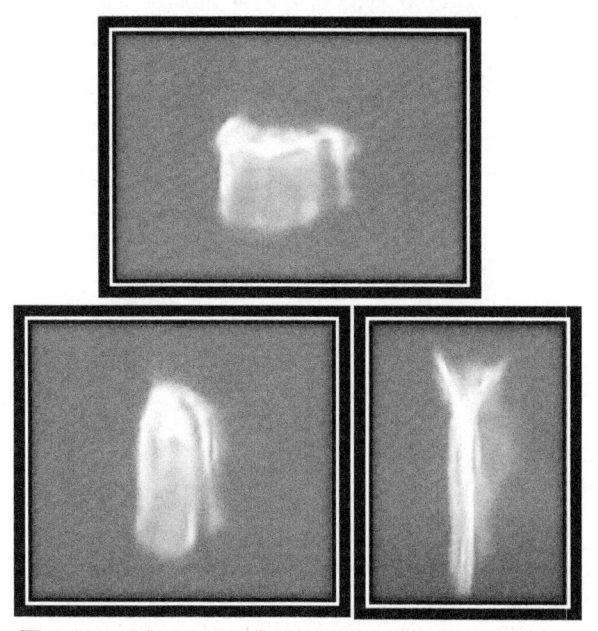

The same object over a few seconds; video taken by a German tourist in July 2021 from an airliner at high altitude

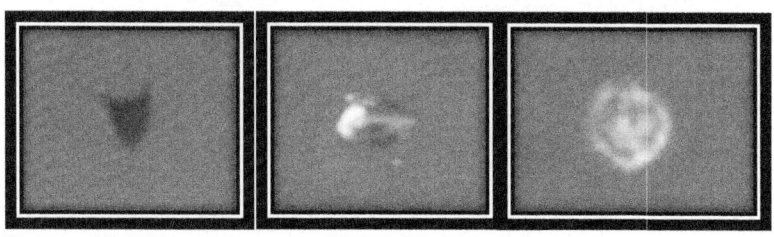

From an F-18 jet, off the coast of Virginia, three photos of the same object within seconds: Travel Channel

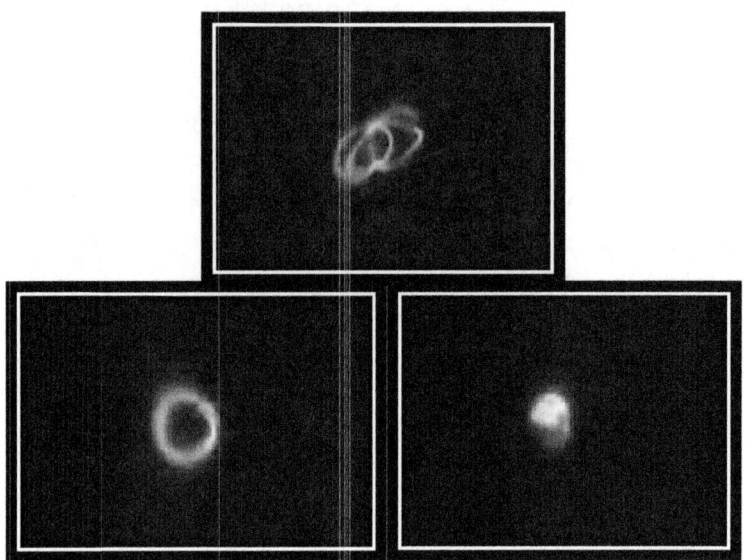

Filmed over Palermo, Italy, 1978; the object changed radically over seven seconds: History Channel

You can see further examples of these antic entities—seeming more creature than craft—on the Plasmoid Anomalies Study Group YouTube channel and at UFOExplorations.com.

1.4 Up close and personal

In order to achieve the sharpest focus on our subject, we also need to value testimonials by "contactees" and "abductees," controversial as these sources may be. I believe most of them are telling the truth. Here again, though, as in the case of the craft themselves, I'll be limiting myself to the easy part, the leading edge, the phenomenology of the encounters as they first unfold; it's here that the experience resonates most tellingly with (other) spiritual/psychic phenomena. I'll leave it for others to ponder the subsequent reported sequence of events—medical procedures, genetic harvesting, and forced sexual linkages.

John E. Mack also believed the witnesses. He was a psychiatrist, Harvard professor, and Pulitzer Prize-winning author when he began charting the landscape of contact and abduction. Through hundreds of in-depth interviews from 1989 to 2004, Mack learned of many consistent features of the experience from people who had never compared notes with others or been exposed to the UAP media content so pervasive today.

Typically, a person is in bed at home or in a car when they become aware of a bright light, a humming sound, strange bodily vibrations, or full paralysis. There appears a nearby craft (characteristics vary) and one or more humanoid figures, usually the small gray beings now familiar to us. Then, the person is "floated" (the most common verb used) against their will directly through matter—walls, doors, windows, or car roofs—and will often notice that the Grays, too, are effortlessly defying gravity, escorting the person. Some hours later, after being subjected to the series of further measures aboard the craft, they find themselves suddenly back in bed or sitting in their car by the side of the road.

I recommend two documentaries: "The Visitors" on TravelChannel.com and "Experiencers: John E. Mack, M.D." on YouTube.

In Chapter 6, I'll feature rich descriptions of the initial transitional phase of these kidnappings, in the experiencers' own words. In Chapters 2, 3, 4, and 5, it's necessary to lay the groundwork in the areas of physics, cosmology, and psychic/spiritual research.

Chapter 2
"There is Nothing Else...":
The Primacy of Fields, the Illusion of Distance

The laws of physics are not about action at a distance, they are local. *All needed information is contained nearby. Everything touches everything else and communicates to its nearest neighbors.*
— Sean Carroll, theoretical physicist

overview

- Introducing *quantum field theory*, the most fundamental explanation of physical reality yet developed. This is the shortest chapter but the most important in terms of cosmology and the nature of matter, which will frame our later consideration of consciousness, which will in turn frame our discussion of UAPs.
- Don't let the q-word frighten you; we'll steer clear of formulas and multi-dimensional models. In fact, quantum field theory shows reality to be surprisingly comprehensible, even by a non-scientist such as myself.
- The main point about fields is that they *unify*. As we see in the Sean Carroll passage above, everything they contain is *directly* in touch with everything else they contain; this is the key insight.

2.1 The mystery of quantum entanglement
You will have heard about this wildly counterintuitive aspect of nature. Electrons, photons, etc., can become inextricably linked, such that the state of one will be correlated with that of the other(s), no matter how far we separate them. *Quantum entanglement* occurs when two (or a group) of such particles are generated together and initially interact. Thereafter, the state of each cannot be described independently of the state of the other(s), including when the particles are separated by a great distance—even by light-years.

The simplest example involves two electrons, which, like all fundamental particles, exhibit what's called *spin*. They can either spin up or spin down, and two entangled electrons will complement one another in this regard; if one spins up, the other will necessarily spin down. When separated by any distance—the current Earthbound experimental record stands at 33 kilometers (20.5 miles)[8]—these particles will continue to behave in perfect sync. It is incorrect to say, as many do, that the one "influences" or "effects" the other, or that they "communicate" faster than light. It would make as much sense to say that one side of a flipped coin, coming up heads, tells or causes the other side to be tails. Instead, changing one spin means that the other spin is automatically changed.

The phenomenon, of course, makes a mockery of the very idea of distance, which is why Einstein could not accept it, sneering that it was illogical "spooky action at a distance." But his formulation was incorrect.

2.2 Action at a distance? False

Isaac Newton and Michael Faraday—in the seventeenth and nineteenth centuries respectively—discovered the gravitational and electromagnetic fields but could not account for how they worked. One magnet can affect another without direct contact? The sun tugs at the Earth from 93 million miles away? We take this for granted today, but when first described, these phenomena seemed positively absurd. What happens *in between* the two objects? No conductive medium could be found; apparently, this was a matter more of magic than of mechanism.

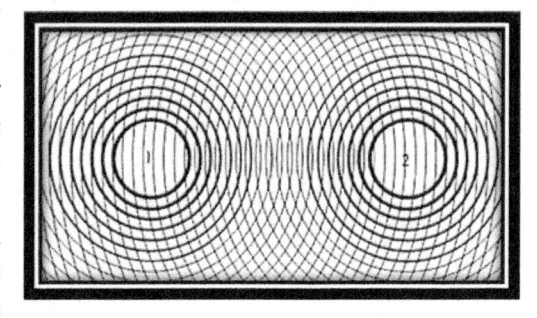

Fast-forward several hundred years and we've replaced the concept of "action at a distance" with that of local influence or "perturbation"; the whole notion of distance has been factored out. First, James Clerk Maxwell recognized that an electromagnetic field exerts a force that propagates not by crossing a gap all at once but by affecting the space right next to it, which then affects its neighboring space, etc.—locallocallocallocal. And then, Einstein gave us a radically new understanding of gravity, a picture of spacetime as a four-dimensional fabric that is warped by objects, more or less so depending on their mass. Objects responding to gravity are responding only to the warping on their very doorstep, which in turn is influenced by the warping on that doorstep's doorstep, and so on. There is no need for mediation because there's no *in between* involved; everything is acting only proximally, in direct contact with its immediate surroundings.

2.3 Quantum entanglement demystified

It turns out that elementary particles are not the most fundamental building blocks of the universe after all, and that, therefore, the coordinated behavior of entangled particles is due to a deeper layer of reality—the deepest we can discern.

"Imagine the entire volume of the universe as filled with different kinds of fluid," advises science writer Arvin Ash.[9] Current physics understands the cosmos as consisting, at bottom, of fluidlike sources of pure potential, *quantum fields*, which give rise to matter. According to *quantum field theory* (QFT), particles come into being as "excitations" of their respective fields—that is, by means of energy. Particles are packets or bundles of energy, each vibrating at its own unique frequency, that pop in and out of existence as a result of ceaseless fluctuations of excitation.

All particles exist as both waves of potential—*virtual particles*—and as these discrete energy packets once actualized. University of Cambridge theoretical physicist David Tong explains that there is, for instance,

> spread throughout space, something called *an electron field*. Ripples of the electron field get tied up into a bundle of energy by quantum mechanics. And this bundle of energy is what we call an electron. Similarly, there is a field for every particle in your body—indeed, every particle in the universe is a tiny ripple of its underlying field, molded into a particle by the machinery of quantum mechanics.[10]

And every elementary particle that makes up matter is part of its own continuous field connecting it to every other such elementary particle, and *potential* such particle, in the universe, and each operating at a unique frequency. Moreover, these fields are constantly moving, vibrating, and interacting.

As we saw above, gravitational and electromagnetic fields exercise their influence by means of uninterrupted contiguity; the same goes for these most fundamental of all possible fields. Theoretical physicist Sean Carroll explains that in light of QFT, "The laws of physics are not about action at a distance, they are *local*. All needed information is contained nearby. Everything touches everything else and communicates to its nearest neighbors."[11]

Two entangled particles "placed" at the far ends of the universe might just as well be pressed side by side because, either way, they are aspects of one continuous object, sharing, and united by, their native quantum field. "Place" itself is a mirage. The discovery of these primordial fields has brought a radical new perspective, so that what may sound like a facile New Age cliché—"Everything is connected"—shows itself instead to be at the very core of hard science.

The implications are all-encompassing, and yet they serve to shrink the "problem space" (parameters of an inquiry) that this book concerns itself with. The concept of *locality* related by Carroll will help us now every step of the way, even when it goes by its alias, *nonlocality*. These apparent opposites speak to a common root—the illusory nature of distance. From the broadest perspective, no object is isolated in a discrete location as opposed to other discrete locations; in this sense, it is *non*local, or call it nonlocal*ized*. You'll often see the term *nonlocal consciousness*, which means that consciousness, too, like everything else, is free from the antiquated notion of distance.

QFT has withstood all theoretical and experimental challenges for nearly a century, ever since first formulated by Paul Dirac in 1927. "When something vibrates, the electrons of the entire universe resonate with it. The greatest tragedy of human existence is the illusion of separateness," Einstein wrote in 1942. And in 1953, Freeman Dyson summed things up neatly in *From Eros to Gaia*.

> Each quantum field fills the whole of space and has its own particular properties. *There is nothing else except these fields*; the whole of the material universe is built of them. Each field manifests itself as a type of

elementary particle. The number of particles of a given type is not fixed, for particles are constantly being created or annihilated or transmuted into one another.[12]

In other words, not only are these universal fields fluidlike in themselves, but their interrelationships are so as well; they flow together and exchange qualities. "The fields talk to each other," Carroll says. "They're rubbing shoulders, and one vibrating field can give its energy away to other fields around it,"[13] and so on and on, shoulder by intimate shoulder. And just as all electrons, all photons, all quarks, etc., are unified by membership in their respective fields, all quantum fields at large are also bound together by mutual compatibility, speaking the same language of energetic vibration. Quantum entanglement narrowly construed—that is, experimentally instigated between or among specially prepared particles—is merely the most blatant embodiment of this broad foundational reality. According to physicist Heinrich Päs, "The entire universe is one quantum object, a single field, linked by entanglement. The classical concept of space doesn't make sense anymore."[14]

2.4 The illusion of distance applies to time as well

For the past hundred and fifteen years, ever since Einstein and Minkowski, space and time have been understood as a single integrated whole—spacetime. Implicit in this cosmology is the obsolescence of the notion of linear time as we experience it here on Earth. In fact, if we remove human awareness from the equation and ask the universe itself, there is no absolute or objective time flow. For reasons too involved to develop right here, this means that, in effect, everthing is happening all at once, which of course carries profound implications for consciousness; see Appendix A: Einstein's Block Universe and the Illusion of Linear Time.

Countless examples of precognition and accurate prophecy grace the pages of history all the way back, and modern physics finally came to understand why. Einstein said, "The distinction between past, present and future is only a stubbornly persistent illusion," and current-day theoretical physicist Carlo Rovelli agrees: "This distinction between past and future is not present in the basic grammar of the world. It comes about only because we have a blurred vision of realty."[15] Those equipped with clearer vision can occasionally see the future and, by touching historical objects, encounter the perpetual presence of the past.

Just one example will suffice here; for an in-depth treatment, see *There Is No Veil*, Chapter 3: Illusions of Time and Space.

In his autobiography, Mark Twain attests to the following incident, recounted by Eric Wargo.

> Before he was Mark Twain, Samuel Clemens was a pilot-in-training on a Mississippi riverboat called The Pennsylvania. He got a job for his younger brother Henry on the same riverboat. Between runs, they were staying with their older sister in St. Louis, and Samuel had a vivid dream of seeing Henry in a steel coffin wearing one of his (Sam's) suits. He saw a woman come into the room and lay roses on the boy's chest.
>
> Three days later, they shipped out on the Pennsylvania, downriver to New Orleans, where Sam got into a fight with the boat pilot, who foisted him ashore so that he missed the run back north. Two days later, Sam got word that there had been a huge boiler explosion that killed many people.
>
> He took the next available riverboat up to Memphis, where he was able to spend time with Henry as he was dying of his burns. The next morning, he entered the room where all the dead were arrayed in their pine coffins except for one; his brother had been given a steel coffin. The nurses had been so impressed with the boy's stoicism the previous night that they'd all pitched in to purchase this superior coffin.
>
> Just as Sam is standing there beholding this scene—seeing that Henry borrowed one of his suits without telling him—a nurse comes in and lays a bouquet of roses on the dead boy's chest.[16]

Chapter 3
Why Consciousness Must also be a Field:
Information and Psychokinesis (PK)

I have to admit that even after thirteen years of directing the [Staford remote viewing] program, still, on many occasions, I would go in to set up an experiment, and I'd ask myself, "What am I doing here? This can't possibly work. There's no mechanism we can think of whereby this could possibly work." And it would work.

—Hall Puthoff, former Director of the Stanford Research Institute

overview

- Highlighting the kinship between fundamental quantum fields and consciousness. Once we recognize the authenticity of psychic phenomena such as telepathy and remote viewing, this kinship becomes quite clear.
- Just as quantum fields bring everything within them into contiguous contact—distance is an illusion—so too does the fundamental consciousness field. All information is immediately available; our only challenge is to resonate with it.
- Moreover, the fundamental consciousness field can interact with these other fields so as to effect change in the observable world of objects; this is called psychokinesis (PK), and recognizing its validity will allow for a more accurate depiction of the UAP enigma than other models of reality can.

3.1 Beyond the five senses

Since time immemorial, humanity has been regularly tapped on the shoulder by hints from a larger reality frame, demonstrating again and again that there's much more to our mental and spiritual life than what's filtered through the five senses. Though ancient examples abound of telepathy, precognition, and remote viewing, the past 150 years have seen the emergence and steady development of the field of parapsychology.

Many of you will be familiar with the plentiful and conclusive evidence for the validity of the various modalities of extrasensory perception. To the rest of you I recommend Russell Targ's *The Reality of ESP: A Physicist's Proof of Psychic Abilities*; Dean Radin's *Entangled Minds*; and the comprehensive 2018 meta-analysis by psychologist Etzel Cardeña, "The experimental evidence for parapsychological (psi) phenomena," which I have included as Appendix B.

The reason consciousness must also be a field is that it exhibits the very same qualities of simultaneous vastness and immanence as the quantum fields; from the viewpoint of any conscious agent within the field, all information—*all*—is local. Regarding the collective of conscious agents everywhere, they are all immediate neighbors. For the conclusively demonstrated phenomena of psychic knowledge, there is simply no other explanation than a consciousness field on the model of the fields governing ordinary matter.

Some see existence as a hologram, in which every part contains the whole, macrocosm within microcosm, as expressed by Rumi's "You are not just the drop in the mighty ocean. You are the mighty ocean in the drop." And this is indeed a fair reflection of QFT, since quantum and consciousness fields also place the universe at our doorstep—immeasurable and intimate both at once.

3.2 Telepathy

Picture a room that looks like a large walk-in freezer but warm and with a comfortable chair—a solid steel, double-walled chamber that shields fully against electromagnetic signals and acoustic noise. Now picture another room, fifty feet away within the same building and containing another chair and a computer screen. The sender(S) sits in front of her screen. The receiver(R) sits in the isolation chamber; all S has to work with are four picture cards showing, say, a horse, a pair of scissors, a mountain, and a car. Ten times during a thirty-minute sending session,

S is shown a randomly selected image (one of the four) on the screen and attempts to mentally convey it to R. R is simultaneously instructed to envision the "target" image and then make his best guess. By pure chance, R should score a "hit" 25% of the time, right?

In *Entangled Minds*, Dean Radin reports that between 1974 and 2004 a total of eighty-eight experiments following this basic protocol were performed, reporting 1008 hits in 3145 trials for an overall hit rate of 32%. This result may seem minor, but keep in mind that its extremely robust replicability over thirty years demonstrates nothing less than a genuine effect unexplainable by current science. Even a 26% outcome, sustained across so many trials, would have demonstrated the same, though less dramatically. *Any* clear-cut evidence of the fundamental consciousness field operating independent of bodily perception would of course establish its existence, even if its informational payload is imperfectly accessed. Radin points out that the 7%-above-chance hit rate represents an unlikelihood of 29,000,000,000,000,000,000 to 1; unlikelihood means "odds against mere chance."[17]

Understand also that these experiments were carried out using thousands of subjects, ordinary people who had shown no salient psychic gifts beforehand. Their striking success speaks, therefore, to a mental capacity widespread among the human population. Others possess it to a much higher degree.

One such savant was Uri Geller. In 1974, his telepathic prowess was sanctioned by *Nature*, the leading science journal in the world.

> At the beginning of the experiment either Geller or the experimenters entered a shielded room so that from that time forward Geller was at all times visually, acoustically and electrically shielded from personnel and material at the target location. Only following Geller's isolation from the experimenters was a target chosen and drawn, a procedure designed to eliminate pre-experiment cueing.

Geller was locked in the shielded room, and then, in another room, experimenters opened a 17,000-page dictionary at random. The first item in the first column that could be drawn was selected as the target image. The inaccuracies in Geller's responses are obvious, but considering the voluminous variety of potential targets—as opposed to just *four*—you'll agree that his attunement is astonishing, more impressive and probative than the 32% hit rate given above.[18]

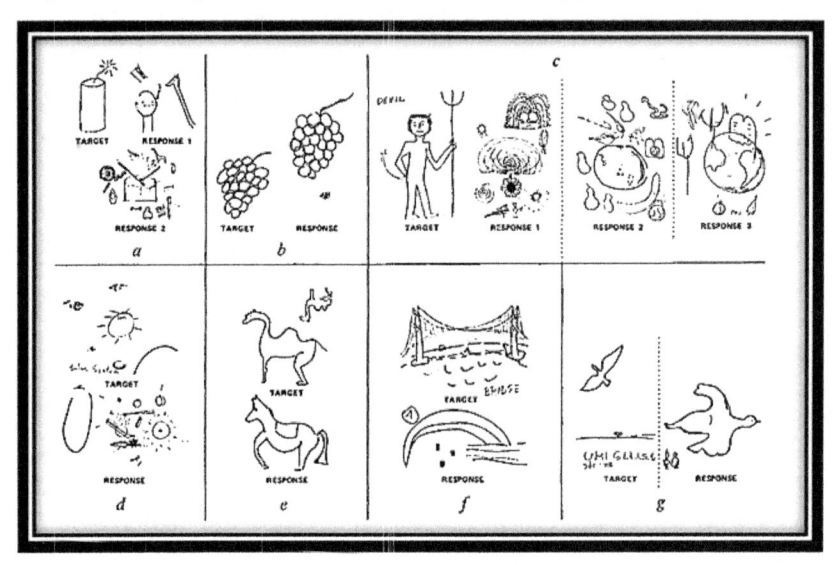

We might wonder why, if our individual consciousnesses are linked into the universal consciousness field, ESP isn't flawless. I think it comes down to the fact that, while on Earth, we are embodied; our wet, three-pound brain serves as an informational receiver and processor, but, given the profound difference between ordinary matter and the type of matter consciousness is made of—and yes, I'll argue that it's a substance, albeit an extremely rarefied one—much is lost in translation.

In their 1979 book *Mind-Reach*, Targ and Puthoff speak of trying to understand the "channel" that allows for remote viewing and telepathic "signaling." This conception has since been proven incorrect, along with the notion that some form of electromagnetic energy is the medium through which psychic phenomena occur. In Ingo Swann and Stephan Schwartz's Project Deep Quest, for instance, remote viewing succeeded even with the target images riding aboard a submarine 1200 feet deep, where any electromagnetic signal would be too attenuated to convey the necessary information. For a thorough discussion of the reasons that consciousness cannot be a function of the electromagnetic spectrum, see Appendix C.

We are all swimming in a sea of interacting fields that span both the universe and our living rooms—rather, we *are* the sea itself; it has no outside. The water droplet of a single brain resonates with the sea variably, but it's never a matter of information *transfer*, of sending or receiving messages between one place and another. That would be to invoke again the obsolete notion "action at a distance."

3.3 Remote viewing

Information access does not represent action at a distance but rather contiguous, neighboring presence. This applies to the fundamental consciousness field as well; just as two entangled particles are actually two aspects of the same object, so too is a remote viewer and her "target." Her challenge is to tune in to this preexisting unity.

For twenty-three years (1972-1995), the United States CIA funded a remote viewing program out of Stanford University and Fort Meade in Maryland. The millions of dollars invested and the longevity of this program— discontinued only with the end of the Cold War and the rise of Internet surveillance—testifies to its success. Co-founded by Russell Targ, a physicist and pioneer in the development of the laser in the 1940s, the Stanford Research Institute recruited

Target   **Remote viewer drawing**

highly gifted psychics who then proved themselves again and again by acquiring targets, such as text written on a sheet of paper miles away, the location (on a map) of a buried object, or even Soviet secrets from across the world.

One celebrated example, declassified years later, is that of a new class of Soviet submarine. In 1979-80, members of the National Security Council had been shown photograps taken by a KH-9 spy satellite that revealed a massive building at the Severodvinsk Naval

Base in Russia. Located 650 miles north of Moscow near the Arctic Circle, this base was under high suspicion by the U.S. intelligence community because of a sudden uptick in activity at the site.

In Remote Viewing Session C54, a sealed envelope was placed on a table in front of SRI remote viewer Joe McMoneagle, their star practitioner. He was asked to provide information about the photo hidden inside. McMoneagle described a huge building "near some kind of shoreline, either a big lake or some bay. It smells like a gas plant," he said, "like there's smelting or melting going on inside the building." He mentioned

> lots of people in funny hats...arc welding...standing on catwalks. They're cutting metal or bending metal, welding metal, shaping metal. Very, very large. There's some kind of ship. Some kind of vessel. I'm getting a very strong impression of propellers. Jesus! This is really mind-blowing. I'm seeing fins, but they're not rocket fins or airplane fins. They're...they look like *shark* fins. I'm getting a stong impression of a huge, coffin-type container. It's like they created part of a submarine to...to fasten this modification to. I think it's like a prototype, perhaps four, five, or six stories tall. I'm asking myself the question, What is this thing? This coffin-like thing? And the answer I keep getting is that it's a weapon.[20]

McMoneagle added that he saw "a concrete structure, like a canal in Holland." That the Soviets would build a submarine inside this building, and not in a dry dock located at the water's edge, seemed to defy logic. The building in the picture was roughly one hundred yards from the shore at the naval yard; nor was any canal visible—only flat, frozen Earth.

Four months after this session, however, new images captured by the satellite over Severodvinsk sent shock waves through the intelligence community. They revealed a massive submarine tethered alongside a dock as well as a channel that had evidently been recently dynomited between the building and the dock. It was now clear that the Soviets had covertly constructed a prototype for an entirely new generation of nuclear-powered, ballistic missile submarine. The Russian code name was *акула*, which translates as *shark*.

Another Stanford psychic, Ingo Swann, is known as "the father of remote viewing." In addition to performing with high accuracy on many terrestrial missions like the one just described, he is credited with having discovered a ring around Jupiter. In 1973, Swann was asked to attempt to see the planet in more detail than had any telescope to date, an assignment he at first rejected; he never wanted to view any target that couldn't be verified. He was told that NASA probes were on their way.

Swann observed a ring like those of Saturn but much subtler and closer to the planet, and he reported that it was made up of dust and tiny asteroids. No astronomer had proposed such a thing, nor did the two Pioneer probes of 1973 and 1974 find any such ring, so his claim was dismissed. Then, in 1979, when Voyager 1 passed by, it clearly identified the feature in question.

The literature on remote viewing is extensive. For starters, I recommend *Mind-Reach* by Russell Targ and Harold Puthoff; *The Stargate Chronicles: Memoirs of a Psychic Spy* by Joe McMoneagle; and *Phenomena: The Secret History of the U.S. Government's Investigations into Extrasensory Perception and Psychokinesis* by Annie Jacobson. There is also a valuable presention on the Area52 channel, "How The CIA Trained Psychic Spies for 20 Years."

3.4 Blindsight

On the more modest end of the same spectrum, but still demonstrating that consciousness is not bound by the five senses, it is possible for a person to receive visual information from right in front of them, without the aid of their ordinary eyes. In *The Watseka Wonder*, E. Winchester Stevens chronicles the 1864 case of Mary Lurancy Vennum, a teenager who, as her eyesight failed, displayed remarkable compensatory perception.

> She could read blindfolded and do everything as readily as when in health by her natural sight. While blindfolded, she took Dr. Trail's encyclopedia, turned to the index, traced the column till she came to the word "blood," then turned to the page indicated and read the subject through. On another occasion she took a box of her letters received from her friends, and sat down, heavily blindfolded by critical, intelligent, investigating gentlemen, then examined and read them without error or hesitancy.[21]

The seminal work on this topic is *Eyeless Sight* by Jules Romains (1924), in which the researcher establishes the authenticity of this capacity of consciousness through careful experimentation—a capacity that turns out to be nearly universal.

A century later now, children and adults are being taught to access this same latent human faculty. I recommend two short documentaries, "The Secrets of Consciousness | Part I: Seeing Without Eyes" on the Thanatos TV EN channel and "Children with Real SuperPowers (Third Eye)" on the Frank Elaridi channel. One young lady explains her experience this way: "I can see with my own light…which is your spirit, third eye…basically the *whole you*."

There are also cases in which people blind from birth verifiably see, for the first time, when their physical bodies are briefly cut out of the loop; see *Mindsight: Near-Death and Out-of-Body Experiences in the Blind* by Kenneth Ring and Sharon Cooper.

3.5 The field itself does the knowing

A common and basic misconception about connecting with information beyond the five senses is that it involves searching and finding. We think by analogy of Internet keywords, triggering the system to instantly traverse the cybersphere and locate the desired content. We envision telepathy, remote viewing, blindsight, or psychic mediumship as a process of reaching out into the infosphere and sifting through potential sources, finally retrieving the nugget she needs.

Instead, however, the operative word is *attunement*; you don't search for and find the information or receive a sent message; the sender(S)/receiver(R) paradigm of telepathy research protocol is incorrect. The "isolation chamber" that R sits in is not actually isolated from S any more than entangled particles light-years apart are isolated from one another. The fundamental consciousness field is ubiquitous and, well, *conscious*; it's ready and able to serve. It works like each of our individual minds does. When we intend to recall a piece of information—presto!—there it is, unless we are insufficiently attuned to what we already know.

This remarkable quality was driven home at Stanford during the 1970s when the SRI researchers refined their remote viewing methodology, winnowing it nearly out of existence. Viewers were given increasingly bare-bones clues to their targets such as mere global latitude-longitude coordinates, concentrating upon which still brought them concrete visions precisely matching the abstractly specified locations.

The field they resonated with was showing itself to be far more user-friendly than ever imagined, requirng no logical bridge from signifier to signified. It was like asking someone with no Spanish to locate a *zapato*. It's not necessary for the individual to know what a certain signifier means if the system itself "knows"; the Spanish language on its own links *zapato* with the thing we wear on our feet.

The process SRI had discovered—or *re*discovered, as it has ancient roots—somehow "knew how to access the requested information, even though the viewer possessed no prior knowledge of, say, the given Earth coordinates," writes Eric Wargo, author of *Time Loops*. "One day, remote viewer Keith Harary flippantly suggested to one of the researchers, 'Why don't you just say the word *target*?' Amazingly, that worked too."[22] For more on the ubiquity of information, see Appendix J.

The only requirement for extrasensory knowing is that the individual first be able to focus and become sufficiently aware of her own resonance, stirred by intention, with the fundamental consciousness field at large. In a psychically gifted person, the gift lies not in establishing a connection; the connection is pre-established. The trick is only to tune in to this connection. She need not engage at the level of the target, just at the level of awareness. Wherever you go, the field is already there, and there, and there—endlessly spawning instances of itself; see Appendix J.

We can now move on to another remarkable facet of reality, one that, like those above, makes sense in light of field theory. You'll recall that the universal quantum fields, which give rise to matter, flow into and affect one another; Sean Carroll tells us that "The fields talk to each other...rubbing shoulders, and one vibrating field can give its energy away to other fields around it." Well, it seems that the fundamental consciousness field is no different. Besides allowing one to directly receive information, it can also act as a physical catalyst, *instilling* information into matter—information calling for noticeable change.

3.6 Psychokinesis (PK) follows naturally

> *Our best guess is that, under certain circumstances, there is a resonance between the information processor that's in the [experimental] device and the information processor in our minds. Somehow, at the level of information, there is a sharing that is accountable for these anomalous effects. The barrier between science and spirt that was artificially erected...must crumble and come down. One should be able to do research on spirit.*
> —Robert Jahn, Princeton University
>
> *The truly fundamental problem [is] that of the relationship between psyche and [ordinary] matter.*
> —Jacques Vallée and Eric Davis[23]

From Plato to Berkeley to Hegel to contemporary philosopher Bernardo Kastrup, countless idealists of all stripes have seen consciousness as operating at the very root of reality; Max Planck famously said, "I regard consciousness as fundamental, matter as derivative from consciousness. We cannot get behind consciousness."

It seems to me that, instead, the fundamental consciousness field plays a leading role but not a foundational one; it's a collaborator field among all those known by the physicists, intimately interwoven with them and able to exert control under certain circumstances. It "talks to" them, resonates with them, both physically influencing and knowing them.

Given this, we'd be able to derive and predict the phenomenon known as *psychokinesis*, or PK, even if we didn't know about it already. PK is typically mischaracterized as "mind over matter." The dualism embedded in that phrase is unsupportable because classifying matter as separate from, *but susceptible to*, some immaterial influence called mind implies that the nonphysical can interact with the physical world, which is absurd. Like the other fundamental fields, the fundamental consciousness field must give rise to its own form of matter and energy; otherwise, it would be nothing and would not exist. We're talking about nature here, after all, and "nature abhors a vacuum."

The type of matter that the fundamental consciousness field gives rise to cannot be the ordinary matter birthed by the known quantum fields because, if it were, we'd have detected it already with our exquisitely ordinary matter-sensitive instruments and correlated it to psychic/spiritual phenomena. On the contrary, we have never been able even to estimate, much less to pinpoint, the concrete principle behind these phenomena. Therefore, another type of matter altogether must be in play behind the scenes; see Chapter 4.

For millennia, the human race took for granted that the world is enchanted, enspirited, endowed with a soulful awareness and agency continuous and compatible with our own. The Scientific Revolution began, in the seventeenth century, to divide us from nature until, by the twentieth, materialism had come to dominate, proclaiming that nothing spiritual or supernatural can be measured, and that therefore it cannot be real.

Then, from 1979 to 2007, the Princeton Engineering Anomalies Research program (PEAR) was finally able to demonstrate with iron-clad experimental rigor that the age-old presupposition was valid, that physical reality and mental reality do indeed interact.

In the PEAR lab, a random event generator (REG) was used, part of "nature" broadly inasmuch as it runs by electrons, essentially a computerized coin-flipper executing one flip per second. Experimental subjects (called "operators") were asked to try to influence the machine's data output by directing conscious intent toward a higher or lower ratio of heads over tails. The Psi Encyclopedia explains,

> In the original "benchmark" REG experiment, the difference between high and low conditions in 2.5 million trials over twelve years of efforts by 91 operators is highly significant with odds of about 15,000 to 1 against chance as an explanation.[24]

Even more dramatic results were obtained by a single psychically gifted operator over 375,000 trails, as shown in this graph.

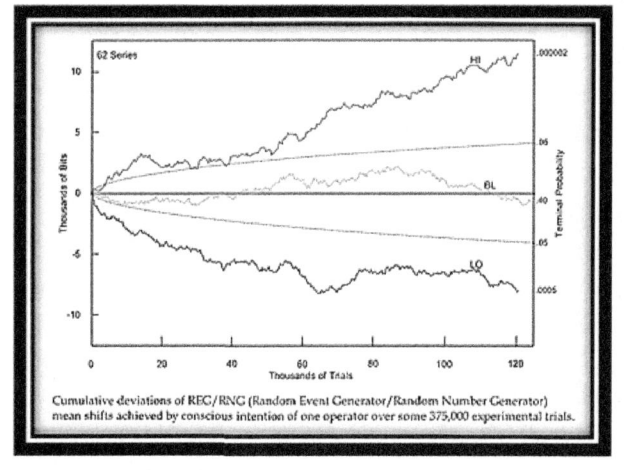

Cumulative deviations of REG/RNG (Random Event Generator/Random Number Generator) mean shifts achieved by conscious intention of one operator over some 375,000 experimental trials.

For a good overview of this PEAR research, see the short documentary "Heretic: Robert Jahn" on the Third Eye Media channel, and for granular detail, there is Jahn and Dunne's *Margins of Reality: The Role of Consciousness in the Physical World*. PK experiments run by Dean Radin have subsequently replicated PEAR's robust findings and taken them further; see his excellent lecture "Science and the taboo of psi" on the Google Tech Talks channel.

Now, it's one thing to produce so-called *micro-PK* effects at the level of electrons and statistics, but what of *macro-PK* effects, such as permanently altering metal? Spoon-bending entails rubbing the utensil with one's fingers while mentally commanding it to soften. When it works, the metal responds far beyond what can be attributed to the heat of friction. In an interview entitled "The Scientific Truth of Psychic Phenomena w/ Dean Radin" on the Unraveling the Universe channel, this world-renowned researcher explains that he focused on the bowl of the spoon, rather than the neck, because here the metal was much thicker.

> It was just like people describe. It feels like putty, and then it just bends over easily, and then it hardens up again instantly, and there it is. How this happens? Total mystery. But it's not imposing anything from the outside, it's doing something that happens way down deep at the microscopic scale and changes the information structure from the inside. Everything is saturated with energy all the time. All you need to do is essentially to turn a switch in the right way and the energy is released.[25]

In the interview "Psychokinesis (PK) with Loyd Auerbach" on the New Thinking Allowed channel, we learn that spoons, hacksaw blades, and other metallic pieces reshaped through conscious intent have been analyzed by metallurgists, who found a structural signature inconsistent with standard mechanical force. "Typically in metal, you see grain boundaries," Auerbach explains, "very specific crystalline structure in the grains of metal, and if you physically bend it, you have fracture and compression." What they found in the metal that had been subjected to PK, on the other hand, was akin to a "*melting* of the grain boundaries, as though intense heat had been applied, even though none had."[26]

Stepping back, we can see that such a transformation is no different at bottom from what occurs within a random event generator under micro-PK influence—particles are being affected by intent. The nub of the issue, as Radin understands, is information, in the broadest sense of the word. Information can be numbers, binary code, written language, etc., but it can also be purely physical, encompassing matter and energy. When it comes to telepathy, remote viewing, and blindsight, our minds resonate with information in whatever form we request, from a bunch of grapes to words in a book to a submarine to a ring around Jupiter. When it comes to PK, the shared vibration simply flows in the other direction, firmly suggesting a revision in "the information structure" of the material at hand. We're not exerting some independent "power of the mind" but rather conspiring with the object itself in common cause—giving it, so to speak, *the idea of changing.*

This same principle is at work in even grander instances of macro-PK, such as when we nullify gravity through levitation.

3.7 Lighter than air

Now, before you dismiss the possibility out of hand, consigning it to the realm of stage magicians and illusionists, consider this: The mere fact that, as we've just seen, consciousness can be intimately and actively in concert with ordinary matter *at all* already marks the leap from a world of arid materialism to one of commingling fields of influence; it's a proof of concept. I would submit that on the far side of this leap, every kindred phenomenon, however apparently miraculous, represents merely a difference in degree, not a difference in kind.

We'll address the gravity issue in the next chapter (section 4.3), but suffice it to say here that this force is not very strong in an absolute sense, as compared to other forces; it only seems so within our limited frame of reference. After all, simply by raising an arm, we are defeating the gravitational might *of an entire planet.*

Leslie Kean, author of *UFOs: Generals, Pilots, and Government Officials Go on the Record*, has also written an excellent book on research into the afterlife. In *Surviving Death*, Kean describes her participation in séances with German physical medium Kai Mügge. "During our first session," she writes, "five of us sat around a plastic garden table, 33.5 inches in diameter and 28 inches high." As a control trial, they first lifted the table manually.

> At Kai's suggestion, Steve and I tried to make it rise straight up while the tabletop remained [perfectly] horizontal. We pressed our hands and knees upward from underneath, but it was impossible to do so. "Any movements we could produce," Steve later wrote, "resulted in table movements that felt obviously different from… genuine levitations, which were slow, buoyant, and weightless."

The Steve she refers to here is University of Maryland philosopher Stephen Braude, author of a probing analysis of the PK phenomenon *The Limits of Influence*, who accompanied Kean on this investigative visit. Later in the session, they experienced the buoyancy of genuine levitation for herself. The table rose "by itself" and remained aloft

> for about fifteen seconds. The table rose at least two and a half feet straight up, and while suspended in the air, it swayed and dipped, gliding as if riding on waves. [When they tried to lower it manually, said another member of the group,] "It was spongy, like pushing down on a spring."[27]

Unfortunately, Mügge's séances take place in near darkness, severely compromising video documentation, as you can see in the image above. Fortunately, however, another gifted individual works in full light.

Ariel Farias leads an ordinary life in Argentina as a family man and textile worker, except for one thing—he is able to persuade tables, via conscious intent, to partially rise off the floor just by concentrating and lightly touching them on top. He says he feels as if he is "merging" with the wood during levitation trials and experiences "sensations like those felt by an airline passenger when the plane takes off."

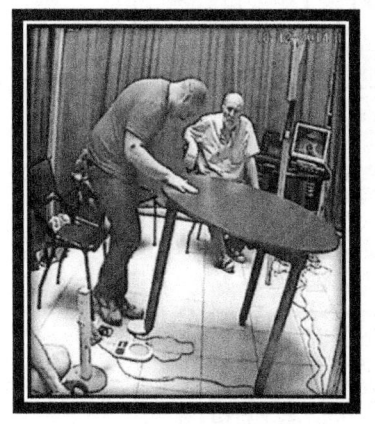

In addition to local researchers running the series of trials in Buenos Aires, Professor Braude was able to attend and vouch for the legitimacy of both the process and the results.

In their peer-reviewed study "Laboratory Research on a Presumably PK-Gifted Subject,"[28] authors Burgo and Gimeno describe the research protocol in great detail. Over eighteen months and twenty-three sessions (2014-2015), multiple cameras were constantly trained on Farias while he performed the levitations. Thirty-one minutes of clear video documentation can be seen on YouTube under the title "Laboratorio de Psicoquinesis: Momentos destacados," with shorter clips also available on the Juan Gimeno channel.

Farias is building upon a rich tradition. From the mid-1800s, "table tipping" became a séance standard, a preferred if time-consuming method of communicating with spirits; the alphabet would be called out, and the table would respond at the right letter. Here (right) is a drawing from 1854.

But more compelling still were moments when tables and chairs would take flight entirely. A tiny fraction were captured visually. Top left is an 1871 engraving, and then historical photographs from 1908 through 1954—generations before Photoshop.

Wish you could actually watch a table lifting fully off the floor instead of just looking at old-timey drawings and photographs? A video called "Harmonic Fellowship of Light Table Levitation" on the Margaret Stark channel shows exactly this, occurring at the home of Neal Rzepowski. Off camera, too, levitation occurs regularly here, just outside the Lily Dale Spiritualist Assembly in Western New York. On June 20, 2023, I attended two séances at Neal's, not on the porch but inside in a darkened room that has hosted thousands of such events over many years. I was lucky enough to witness two object levitations in low light with my own eyes—tin megaphones called "trumpets," which rose to the ceiling untouched by any of us.

A short clip, "Complete Table Levitation" on the Neal Rzepkowski channel, shows another such success.

I'd also highly recommend the interview "Table Levitation with Stephen E. Braude" on the New Thinking Allowed channel.

If you read Appendix B, you may wonder why Etzel Cardeña's round-up of experimental parapsychology results includes micro-PK but not macro-PK, such as levitation. The reason is that the latter doesn't lend itself to standard scientific protocol. Your average study subject off the street cannot do it, nor is it susceptible to statistical analysis; either the table rises or it does not. Most of the time, it does not, unless you are a particularly gifted individual like Ariel Farias, willing to demonstrate in a laboratory, or to participate in the highly conducive context of an experienced, harmonious group or a long-established séance regimen, in which a variety of physical manifestations consistently occur. When you think about it, macro-PK

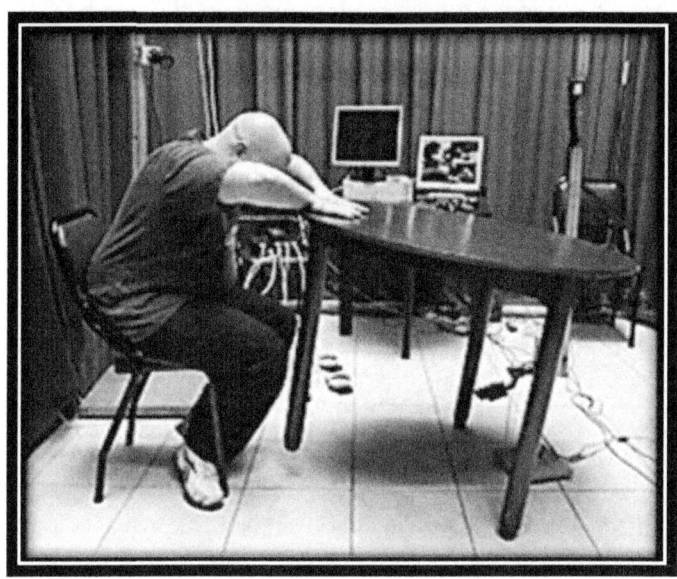

is the kind of phenomenon that requires no more than one "hit"; as Dutch psychiatrist Frederik van Eeden wrote, "All science is empirical science; all theory is subordinate to perception; a single fact can overturn an entire system."
Ariel Farias

Chapter 4
Anti-Gravity without Technology:
Shifting Ratios in a Fluid World

When you can sit in a room and watch objects levitate before your eyes, which I've done many times, and so have many others, there's got to be a physics...a scientific explanation of what is going on to make that happen, and I wish that more scientists were curious about this. This is actually happening. Where's that curiosity?

—Leslie Kean[28]

What we need are some anomalies that would hint at what the nature of dark matter is. In order to learn from new experiences, we must silence the ego of experts who tend to explain away anomalies based on past knowledge. They often raise dust that prevents everyone else from having a clear view. Once the dust settles, we usually have new insights into our cosmic neighborhood.

—Avi Loeb, Harvard theoretical physicist

overview

- Introducing dark matter into the picture, getting a handle on its properties, and beginning to assess its role in paranormal reality.
- I propose a theory to shed light on physical anomalies long documented in history and in parapsychological research. The matter-type ratio theory (MTR) presents a straightforward, nondualistic model wherein the two known forms of matter—ordinary matter and dark matter—collaborate to cause changes that we experience as psychic/spiritual phenomena.
- We revisit the levitation enigma from Chapter 3 and view it through the lens of MTR, then extend the

new model to other psychic/spiritual events such as "apports"—objects appearing "out of thin air"—in preparation for a deeper discussion of UAPs in Chapter 5.

4.1 Ordinary matter and invisible (dark) matter

Although the first evidence for dark matter was discovered in the 1930s, it was in the early 1980s that astronomers became convinced that most of the mass holding galaxies and clusters of galaxies together is invisible.
—"A Brief History of Dark Matter," Joel Primack

Across thousands of years of recorded history—ever since the "first ghosts" in Babylon[30]—the human race has understood that some further variety of experience, some agency operating in a larger reality frame, must exist beyond what our five senses can perceive. We've interacted with its array of uncanny manifestations, which emerge seemingly "out of nowhere" from some invisible, apparently nonphysical (metaphysical) source. It cannot, of course, be *literally* nonphysical. Its provenance and makeup cannot be *nowhere* and *nothing*; they are *something*, and when "something happens," it automatically declares itself to be real. According to physics, "real" is only matter and energy; even the supposed vacuum of space is not actually empty. My outlook, too, is nondualistic: There is not matter/energy *and then something else*. Whatever has been causing "supernatural" effects all this time with no conventional explanation must itself be matter and energy of some type.

But what type?

While religious traditions exalted otherworldly, supernatural forces and personages, evolving science (natural philosophy) sought a more concrete explanation, positing an unseen but decidedly physical medium pervading the cosmos that they labeled *aether*—a catch-all concept to account for any phenomena lacking a known natural cause.

Even into the early twentieth century, physicists still clung to this notion until their attempts to detect aether ran out of steam. Modern science had finally banished this quaint holdover from ancient times.

Not so fast.

Just a half century later, and this time supported by hard evidence, our evasive old friend rose again in the ethereal form of *dark matter*, so much less dense as to escape direct detection by current scientific instruments but plentiful enough nonetheless—making up 85% of all matter—to gravitationally affect whole galaxies and galaxy clusters throughout the cosmos. These massive groups of stars spin much faster and more coherently than would be possible given the gravitation effect of ordinary matter alone, and so astronomers were forced to infer vast "halos" of unseen matter surrounding and suffusing each group.

Since 1986, and much more earnestly since the turn of the century, physicists have gone to extreme and expensive lengths to detect even a single particle of this mystery substance—thus far with zero success.

The two matter types are complementary, having collaborated primordially in the formation of all stars and galaxies, and afterward in those galaxies' continued coherence and rate of spin. Without stars, of course, there would be no habitable planets.

This image, showing our galaxy and its dark matter halo, makes it look like the substance gives way to empty space at a certain point. In fact, however, taking a much broader view, cosmologists have found that it forms a "cosmic web" between and among galaxies and galaxy clusters throughout the universe. This surprising pervasiveness represents a primordial "scaffolding"; it's only thanks to dark matter that suns and galaxies were able to form in the first place. Suns are formed when vast clouds of dust and gas—*solar nebulae*—collapse due to gravity. And then, the eventual galaxies containing billions of suns and planets are structured and held together by their halos. Since dark matter contributes the great majority of gravity to the overall system, none of this development could have occurred without it, and our universe would be a place of much less order, much less information—and, of course, no life.

Even here on Earth, as NASA astronomer Phil Plain puts it, "Dark matter surrounds and penetrates us. We're living in a sea of it." And yet, science has thus far utterly failed in the quest to detect even one IM particle. No shortage of advanced and costly technology has been thrown at the problem; nor do we want for theories as to the nature of this sneaky stuff.

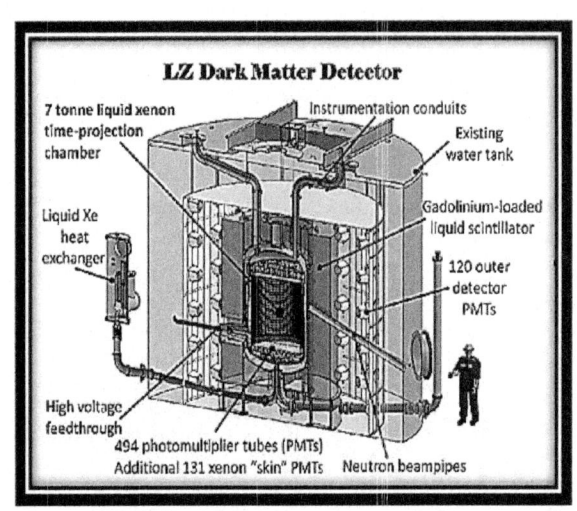

A cutaway rendering of the massive LUX-ZEPLIN (LZ) detector was installed in 2020 a mile deep near Lead, South Dakota. The central detector is filled with 10 metric tons of purified liquid xenon that produces flashes of light and electrical pulses in particle interactions. An array of photomultiplier tubes is designed to amplify and measure these particle signals.

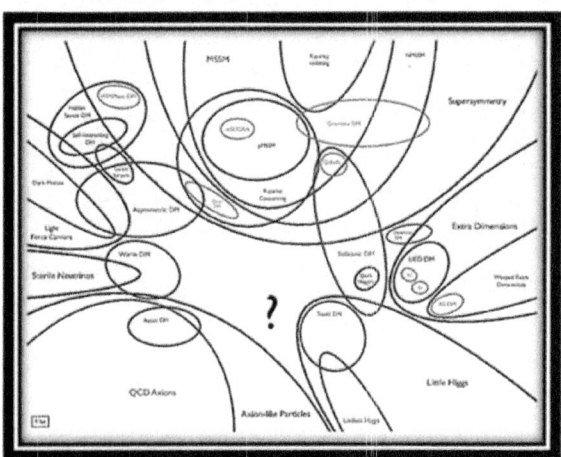

Venn diagram of the wealth of competing theories to explain dark matter

In recent years, we've gotten used to hearing about this unexplainable aspect of reality, but take a moment to actually absorb the situation. Existence is apparently made up of two—*and only two*—

UAPs and the Afterlife 49

types of matter. One is familiar, while the other is entirely unseen and yet far outweighs the familiar type; it is the majority matter.

This strains comprehension. Look around your room and try to grasp the fact that most of what's in front of you is not what you think. Nor is most of what's inside you. We know its effect on the cosmic level, but what is it doing here at our own modest scale? What role is it playing when everything is normal? What role might it play in any *para*normal events that suddenly occur and that have no explanation—*and never have had*—within the ordinary-matter framework?

From here forward, I will call ordinary matter OM and dark matter IM for "invisible matter"; this avoids any confusion with darkness in our everyday sense and any association between "dark" and negativity.

Do we know anything more about IM than its gravitational tug?

The prevailing view has been that IM must be of such extremely low density that, while it does force OM to organize on the macro scale, it cannot itself clump together to form complex structures; that is, it is not capable of self-interaction.

However, credible theorists are not so sure. Whole galaxies have been discovered that are mostly composed of this substance; see for instance "Invisible Dark Matter Galaxy Found..." on the Anton Petrov channel. And Harvard astrophysicist Avi Loeb, much in the news of late for his UAP research and analysis of interstellar objects, remains agnostic on IM self-interaction, noting that, if true, it

> would allow for the possibility that there are "dark atoms" that emit "dark radiation" and condense into "dark stars" and "dark planets" that support "dark chemistry" that leads to "life-as-we-do-not-know-it." In such a case, the answer to Fermi's question: "Where is everybody?" might be: "You are blind to most of them."[31]

4.2 A short course in mass and density

So, just how much of this stuff surrounds and penetrates you right now?

The universe at large contains about six times more IM than OM, but where it interacts with whole galaxies, the proportional asymmetry rises steeply. The consensus estimate is that our Milky Way rotates such that it must be governed by about 95% IM; that's a 20/1 ratio.

But when it comes to an individual solar system and its planets, the case becomes less clear. Estimates vary wildly, but a 2022 study by the Royal Astronomical Society puts the ratio on Earth and in our immediate neighborhood at about 1/1.[32] Since this is the most conservative credible figure I can find, I'll go with it.

Now, before you start trying to envision an even-steven cohabitation between IM and OM particles, take this next piece on board. The 50% IM estimate refers only to its *mass*, whereas *density* is something else entirely. Mass is the amount of matter in an object (solid, liquid, or gas), while density is how much space that mass takes up (its volume) *in relation to* its amount of matter (its mass). For instance, the density of a cubic foot of air containing X number of molecules is twice that of a two-cubic-foot volume of air containing the same X number of molecules.

The density of IM is almost unfathomably lower than that of OM. According to Jillian Scudder, Assistant Professor in Physics & Astronomy at Oberlin College, "A single grain of birch pollen [0.025 of a millimeter] floating alone in a cubic kilometer of space would contain twenty times more mass than there would be of dark matter in that same volume."[33]

How can we get our minds around such a proposition? A cubic kilometer is 3281 feet across. Let's go inside. We walk from wall to wall in 2405 casual steps. Now where is that birch pollen grain anyway? I find it and give it to you. You see it's a teeny-tiny black dot in the palm of your hand—about the size of the period at the end of this sentence. And yet, the dot outweighs, *twenty times over*, the IM filling our cube.

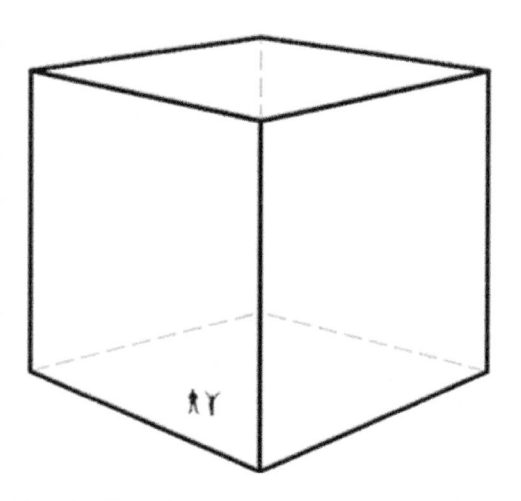

For visibility, I've greatly exaggerated our sizes.

Now leaving our thought experiment, eyeball your personal space again. A person's cosmology determines how she sees her room. Try to envision its true contents using the above information. Squinting might help. For the total mass of your room's IM to equal the amount of its OM mass, how many more IM particles must be involved? They compose a matter type astronomically more rarefied, and yet by sheer numbers alone they compensate for this enough to match the mass of their drastically higher-density counterparts.

From now on, then, let's think of IM not just as the majority matter but as the *vast* majority matter in terms of particle population. In your mind's eye, you can watch the air in front of you, IM particles swarming in their immeasurable multitudes, in their trillions, around every few molecules of ordinary air—oxygen and nitrogen. The same is true of that chair across the room; it may appear quiescent, just sitting there, but in fact it is teeming with vibrating particles, bursting with energy. And the two matter types, though co-located in the action space called "chair," are vibrating at altogether different rates. In nature, at the submicroscopic level, a particle's frequency—its vibration rate—is inversely proportional to its mass. The hydrogen atom, for example, is the lightest OM atom in the universe, and thus its frequency is the highest.

Only try to imagine, then, the vibrational heights of IM particles incalculably lighter than hydrogen.

And we're not done yet. We need to keep on puzzling until, like the Grinch, our "puzzler is sore." We've been thinking in shorthand. Longhand will loosen up the case, allowing for more improvisational flow within the material world. Recall that particles are not the bottom line. As we saw in Chapter 2, reality is based in fluidlike quantum fields that give rise to particles. In other words, what's before you in your room right now is not primarily a pointillist collection of individual bits but rather a dynamic confluence, a charged solution ready for anything—pregnant with pure potential. And "solution" may serve in its other sense, too, letting us solve many vexing enigmas.

In Chapter 3, then, I showed how consciousness seems to behave like any OM quantum field: In each OM field, all of its information is intimately bound up together, nullifying distance; in the IM field, too, all information is unified and conserved. And the latter can engage any or all of the former, resulting in what we know as PK.

Since consciousness is something rather than nothing, and since, as far as we can tell, there are only two categories of something, consciousness must be located in the category of IM. I'm not saying that consciousness and IM are one and the same; I think that the fundamental consciousness field *produces* IM just as the other fundamental quantum fields produce electrons, quarks, and all other elementary particles.

For some backstory on the concept of a universal, invisible substance besides ancient aether, see Appendix G.

4.3 Back to floating furniture: the buoyancy explanation

> *If [after long meditation practice] a Bhikkhu should desire, Brethren, to exercise one by one each of the different Iddhis...to become visible, or to become invisible; to go without being stopped to the further side of a wall, or a fence, or a mountain, as if through air; to penetrate up and down through solid ground, as if through water; to walk on water without dividing it, as if on solid ground...*
> —Buddhist, *Akankheyya sutra*, 3rd century BCE

No small-m materialistic approach has ever produced the foggiest notion of how PK works. Let's see if our capital-M Materialism—which includes both matter types—can lend a hand.

IM and OM obviously collude on the scale of galaxies, but on that of elementary particles, they have not seemed to, at least thus far within our grandiose subterranean detectors.

But nobody is talking about the middle ground where changes occur—such as macro-PK—that mainstream science has not learned to pay attention to. Physicists never hunt for any potential IM influence right under their noses, at the level of objects and atmospherics on the human scale. I'm contending that not only does this influence exist but that it is in constant operation, though ordinarily unnoticed—until something bizarre emerges "out of thin air."

Avi Loeb observes that "we need some anomalies that would hint at...the nature of dark matter," and indeed, what could fill that bill better than macro-PK phenomena that throw a monkey wrench into the known laws of physics?

When a table defies gravity beneath Ariel Farias's hands in Argentina, when Leslie Kean witnesses another one suspended midair in Germany and feels its resistant "buoyancy" as she presses down on top, or when five people on a porch in Western New York coax a table up off the floor "by itself," we have to put on our common-sense thinking caps. How might an ordinary object suddenly become lighter than air?

The answer does not involve electromagnetism; Farias's repeated levitations were checked for this; see Appendix C. Nor does advanced theoretical physics play a role, with its multiple dimensions, zero point energy, warp drives, and traversable wormholes.

The situation is far simpler than that, more commonsensical. The operative quality here is *buoyancy*. Air, like any gas, is a kind of fluid.[34] Objects can be buoyant in water, and helium balloons are buoyant in air. And what is buoyancy a function of? Density. The less dense an object, the greater its buoyancy in a fluid. Therefore, whatever is happening to an object just before it "defies gravity" must be reducing its density.

Macro-PK is not accomplished by means of some magic force field emanating from the participants. We recall Dean Radin's intuition that when his spoon became putty-like between his fingers, this was not caused by "imposing anything from the outside, [but rather by] doing something that happens way down deep at the microscopic scale and changes the information structure from the inside."

We can learn much from two celebrated physical mediums of the past; a *physical medium* is one around whom macro-PK events consistently occur, as opposed to a *mental medium*, who is able to convey accurate information from spirits.

A century and a half ago, renowned British chemist Sir William Crookes found that under the conscious influence of D. D. Home (1833-1886)—the Scottish physical medium often cited as the most potent and rigorously studied of the nineteenth century—objects would not only lose weight and rise entirely off the floor but also, at Home's will, *gain* so much weight that men could hardly budge them anymore.

"I have seen on five separate occasions," Crookes writes in his classic *Researches in the Phenomena of Spirituality* (1874),

> objects [changing] in weight from 25 to 100 lbs. [such that] I and others present could with difficulty lift them from the floor. Wishing to ascertain whether this was a physical fact, or merely due to a variation in the power of our own strength under the influence of imagination, I tested with a weighing machine the phenomenon on two subsequent occasions. On the first occasion, the increase of weight was from 8 lbs., normally, to 36 lbs., 48 libs., and 46 lbs., in three successive experiments tried under strict scrutiny. On the second occasion, in the presence of other observers, I found the increase of weight to be from 8 lbs. to 23 lbs., 43 lbs., and 27 lbs., in three successive trials.[35]

Forty years later, a sixteen-year-old Irish girl, Kathleen Goligher, found that she could also radically alter the weight of objects, and could do this, like Home, in both directions. In 1914, Dr. William J. Crawford, a mechanical engineer, began investigating Goligher's remarkable mediumship, which included floating objects. Over two and a half years, Crawford attended eighty-seven sittings with the Goligher family's séance circle.

For our purposes, his work with scales deserves special attention. No one, it seems, had thought of levitation as a holistic system and sought to measure it as such until Crawford put the medium *herself* on a scale. When, at her mental command, she caused a sixteen-pound table to rise from the floor, the machine showed that Goligher simultaneously gained that same weight.

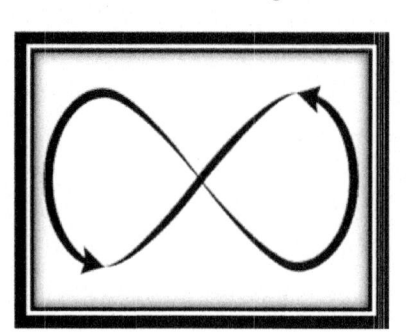

This remarkable transference effect was repeated and extensively documented (Crawford, 1916; Crawford, 1918). The girl was able, also, to significantly increase an object's weight—just like Home in the description above—and each time, her own weight decreased by the same amount.

It seems that in the levitation process, we see a transaction—a dynamic, reciprocal flow of matter types. In *The Reality of Psychic Phenomena* (1916), Crawford writes,

> I think there can be little doubt that it is actual matter temporarily taken from the medium's body and put back at the end of the séance.[36]

If we could put on glasses that showed reality more accurately, we'd see there's little distinction between object and air; "solid" objects would reveal themselves as just another variety of space.

Given how long macro-PK has been conscientiously researched, and the wholesale lack of any OM-related explanations defined or even suggested, it would be illogical not to look instead to the *only other* sector of reality on our radar screen.

4.4 The matter-type ratio theory (MTR)

> *The fabric of reality is like a woven material. There's a warp and a woof, and it's the intermixing of the two that creates the universe as we perceive it. The warp and woof is matter/energy and consciousness in a complementary relationship. One without the other is not enough.*
>
> —Dean Radin

It seems reasonable to propose an integral role for this other sector of reality—IM—and to see our experience as governed by the *ratio* between IM and OM. I think that in our usual daily experience, when nothing "impossible" or "otherworldly" is afoot, a default ratio obtains, maintaining familiar conditions. But our world is always pregnant with possibility, and occasionally, while the basic ingredients hold steady, the *recipe* can suddenly change, the matter-type ratio shifting, as when a table floats, a UAP materializes over a cornfield, or a spirit appears at the foot of your bed. The fundamental stuff of reality—formatted by the IM/OM collaboration—is endlessly improvisational, kaleidoscopic, information always poised to rewrite itself on demand.

And what causes these changes? What's the catalyst? What turns the kaleidoscope?

Conscious intent. Depending on the aims of the conscious agent in any given situation, density can either increase or decrease inside an object or in the atmosphere of a room. It's easy to envision how density can decrease—ultra-thin IM locally proliferating—but harder to grasp the opposite. Any modulation, however slight, of the prevailing 50/50 integration of the two matter types will cause noticeable change. A conscious agent may choose to focus on a single object, withdrawing some of its IM mass, as when a physical medium wills a table to become heavier or when a spirit "materializes"/densifies by upping its quotient of visible or palpable OM, utilizing available raw materials; see Appendix E. The fundamental consciousness field can interact with any OM fields whose offspring particles it may require for a specific project. Working at full potential, it's a master orchestrator; see section 4.9.

4.5 Confirmation from another angle

A different form of macro-PK reinforces the case, exhibiting the same inside-out effect, in which the basic constitution of an object—its physical information—is revised from within, as in Radin's spoon-bending.

Ever since the 1849 birth of Spiritualism in Hydesville, New York, one of the most salient manifestations of spirit presence has been knocks, often called "raps," on walls and tables. But it was not until 2010 that we learned of the highly atypical nature of this percussion. Barrie G. Colvin analyzed recordings of alleged poltergeist raps obtained over a forty-year period at various locations. The earliest was obtained by a physician at Sauchie, Scotland, in 1960, and the most recent came from a case at Euston Square, London, in 2000. Ten clips were preserved on ten different recording devices.

In contrast to a knock produced normally, say by striking a wood surface with one's knuckles, each of the ten paranormal recordings, when subjected to acoustical analysis, shows an atypical sound signature. The difference is seen in spectrogram waveforms. The signature of a typical knock starts strongly and decays quickly. The loudest part of the sound—the highest energy—is seen right at the beginning, at impact.

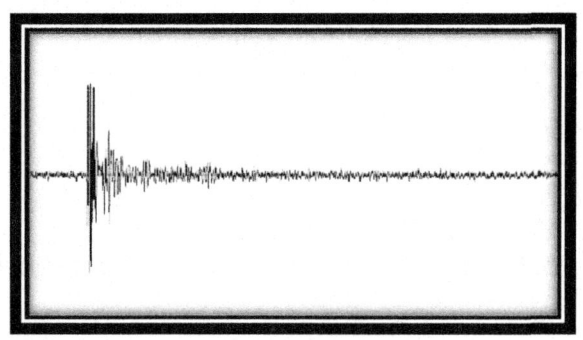

Waveform of a knuckle striking a tabletop

In the case of an alleged poltergeist rap, however, the highest energy concentration occurs near—but not *at*—the beginning. The process starts relatively quietly and works up to a maximum before it then decays.

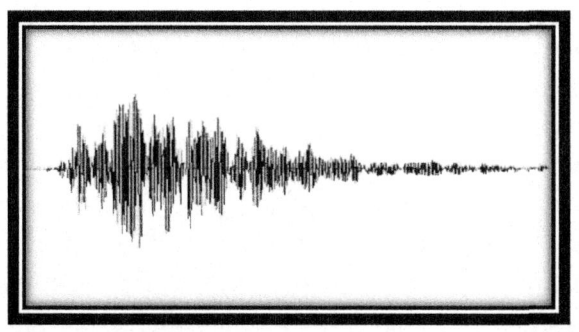

Waveform of alleged poltergeist rap, Sauchie case, 1960

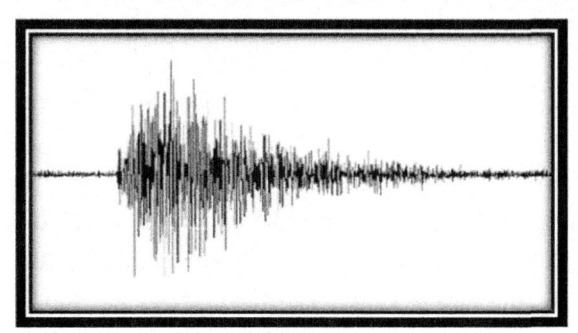

Waveform of alleged poltergeist rap, Ipiranga case, 1973

This delay effect has been seen in all ten of the cases studied. We can note the differing levels of energy transferred to the wood substrate, represented by the density of the signatures.

The consistent profile indicates that the sounds did not originate at the surface of the material; Colvin concludes that these raps on wood are not actually raps *on* wood at all. Rather, they

> appear to involve the buildup of a stress *within a material*, culminating in an audible sound when the level of stress reaches a specific magnitude, and the stress is relieved. The…precise physics of this mechanism is unknown. They appear to develop from within the molecular structure of the substrate.[37]

Our two matter types are co-located; everything in our familiar world is constituted—throughout its "information structure"—of both IM and OM, but their proportions are not static. The "precise physics" of spirit raps, I propose, entails an abrupt shift in the IM/OM ratio within the wood of wall or table, etc., spiking IM with pinpoint accuracy, thus causing a localized drop in density, internal stress, and finally an audible report. In the case of full levitation, too, the proportion of IM to OM must be enhanced, but this time throughout the object until it achieves positive lift. The difference is akin to that between a laser beam and a floodlight.

But how? By means of conscious intent, whether deployed from an incarnate or a discarnate (formerly biological) mind. Remember that consciousness is a fundamental field that interacts with the other (OM) fundamental fields as described by quantum field theory, so why shouldn't it be every bit as animated and animating as the others? We'll get into the implications for UAP research in Chapter 5.

4.6 The meaning of cold and "psychic breeze"

The relationship between matter-type ratios and microclimates is particularly interesting and intimately related to the foregoing.

"Cold spots" are common in haunted houses. Nor is the phenomenon merely subjective; it registers on thermometers. "We've had temperature drops of up to ten degrees that manifest within seconds," said Mark Keyes, director of the Pennsylvania Paranormal Association, in just one of countless researcher confirmations.

But why should an IM/OM ratio shift cause cold? Because IM is so much less dense than OM that when it locally proliferates, it disperses OM air, and the kinetic energy (heat) of the affected air molecules promptly declines with the increased distance between them.

The same microclimate conversion was familiar within authentic Spiritualist séances of the nineteenth century, including those of D. D. Home. Again and again, it coincided with the onset of spirit manifestations, reminding one of the arrival of a weather front. As documented by Julie de Gloumeline in *D. D. Home: His Life, His Mission* (1888),

> Ice-cold blasts of air were felt by the sitters drifting across their hands, so frequent a forerunner of other phenomena. Presently, as to the ear it seemed, exactly in the centre of the table, came a tap, tap, tapping, regular, continuous, and prolonged; on hearing which Mr. Home announced that he was now nearly sure we should have manifestations of some sort.

She quotes Sir William Crookes on the recurring inrush.

> Interesting to Mr. Crookes was the remarkable phenomenon that thousands before him had noted at séances with Mr. Home. "These table movements," he attests, "are generally preceded by a peculiar cold air, sometimes amounting to a decided wind. I have had sheets of paper blown about by it, and a thermometer lowered several degrees. On some occasions...the cold has been so intense that I could only compare it to that felt when the hand has been within a few inches of frozen mercury."[38]

By the same token, in the system of exchange that facilitates levitation, as the two matter type ratios cycle between levitator and object, both hot and cold are generated. The researchers studying Ariel Farias reported that

> Ariel usually mentioned feeling an intense heat in his hands before and during the production of the phenomenon. This is especially curious in view of the fact that observers consistently found Ariel's hands and forearms to be noticeably colder than their own. To examine the matter further, two temperature sensors of

> tiny mass were developed, one for each hand. The temperature of the palms became stabilized during the test at 32,7°C for the left hand and 33,1°C for the right. Normal body temperature varies between 36° and 37°.[39]

That's a more than five-degree Fahrenheit chill-down on the surface of the man's skin, whereas *within* his arms and hands, he felt an "intense heat." The reciprocal matter-type flow registers side by side.

This striking dual effect is found as well in traditional energy healing, which makes sense because an equivalent collaboration is taking place, this time between practitioner and recipient. In a Reiki session, for instance, both participants will experience a transfer of IM and OM, perceived by turns as higher and lower temperature. According to the International Association of Reiki Professionals,

> hand temperature may change as [one is] giving Reiki treatments. These changes range from burning hot to icy cold. Sometimes, the practitioner's and the recipient's perceptions of the temperature will be different. For instance, as you are giving Reiki, you may feel that you're burning up, but your recipient may feel coolness from your touch. Or it may be that you are experiencing cold hands, while the recipient may comment on the warmth of your hands.[40]

For an overview of the subtle energy variously called *qi, prana, ka, ruh, astral body, energy body*, etc., and its relationship to our main themes, see Appendix D. And for a short historical survey of Western theories to account for this unseen agency, see Appendix G.

Two further, often-reported haunting or visitation effects are the slamming of doors and disturbing physical symptoms. The first can be explained as the result of a sudden pressure differential between rooms, aka psychic breeze. The second is akin to an "airplane headache"; a passenger feels as though a vise is being applied to her skull. This sensation is due to a reduction of air pressure as the plane ascends—an imbalance created between the lower pressure in the cabin and the higher pressure still in her frontal sinuses. Witnesses to spirit manifestations also frequently report their eardrums "popping" and, like mountain climbers, may experience symptoms of altitude sickness, such as dizziness, cold sweat, and shortness of breath. I would advise "ghost hunters" to include altimeters or barometers in their tool kits.

4.7 Apports raise the stakes

> *It seems impossible to get it through your heads that objects can pass from an etheric to another level of matter and will then appear to materialize there. This is a perfect analogue witnessed in the séance room. Not only do human forms materialize, but solid objects appear "miraculously," and often these are brought from long distances. You call them* apports. *Well, these "saucers" that puzzle you so much come out of an etheric world also and can return to it. The purpose of these visitors is simply to compel your attention, to wake you up.*[41]
>
> —The deceased Charles Lingford, speaking through medium Mark Probert, 1947

We can now proceed to an even more mind-boggling phenomenon, but one also comprehensible within the MTR framework. As when we made the leap from micro- to macro-PK, it's important here to bear in mind the distinction between kind and degree. Once we grant the sheer versatility of matter—that this *kind* of thing is possible— we can then stretch to accept a greater *degree*, a wider range of effects that represent creative variations on a theme.

For as long as human beings have been observing psychic/spiritual phenomena, these have occasionally included objects appearing "out

Just a few of more than 100 apports received by the Scole group

of thin air." During the height of the Spiritualist movement (1855-1940), these objects came to be called *apports*, French for "to bring." Séances led by elite physical mediums—such as D. D. Home, Eusapia

Paladino, and Alec Harris—would receive all manner of small objects delivered to their locked séance rooms. In the mid-1990s, the Scole séance group in England experienced the sudden materialization of coins, jewelry, medallions, flowers, and silverware.[42]

I heartily recommend *The Scole Experiment* by Grant and Jane Solomon, which comprehensively chronicles one of the most sustained, innovative, and evidentially significant projects in the history of psychic/spiritual research; Daniel Drasin's documentary "Scole: The Afterlife Experiment" is another excellent source.

In one memorable episode, a newspaper thudded down onto the séance table, apparently coming straight from the past and skipping all the days in between—an original copy of the *Daily Express* of Monday 28th May 1945. It was printed on paper of the type used in the early- and mid-1940s, but it was in mint condition. There was no sign of the usual yellowing that would have occurred if it had existed since 1945; see section 2.4.

Investigator Montague Keen writes, "We took it to the leading research station on paper and printing, PIRA, and it was absolutely clear from their report that, first of all, it was printed on letter press, which has been out of existence since the early 1970s. Secondly, it was newsprint produced during wartime, which lacked certain chemicals" unavailable due to rationing. "This was the genuine article, appearing fifty years after its production." Just a few weeks later, the aported newspaper, though carefully stored away from light and air, had turned yellow.

Where do such things come from? And how is this feat accomplished?

In *The French Revelation: Voice to Voice Conversations with Spirits Through the Mediumship of Emily S. French*, researcher Edward C. Randall relates an incident personally witnessed at a sitting with Mrs. French in May of 1897.

> There was no movement of Mrs. French's body, but flowers came apparently from every direction, even from the ceiling, striking me on the head, face, chest, back and side, falling on the table and around us in great profusion. I immediately opened the door and hurriedly called others of my household to see the display. We found upon the table, chairs, and carpet upwards of one hundred pure, white sweet peas, fresh, with dew on the petals. The stems had been twisted off.

The MTR meets instances of such high strangeness with the logic of proportion. An object undergoes a diffusion of its OM particles, an influx of IM particles, until it vanishes; upon delivery, the process is reversed. "At a later time," Randall continues,

> I asked how such a demonstration, so at variance with physical laws, was possible. I was told that no law had been violated, but that physical laws that mankind had not yet discovered had been used, that spirit people took sweet peas from a garden where they grew in too great abundance, changed their vibratory conditions, as we change water into steam, conveyed them in this state into the room, altered the vibration back again into its primary stage, which restored the flowers to their original condition and color. Then they threw them on and about me and Mrs. French. They did this to show me their strength and to demonstrate a vibratory law.[43]

Outside of the séance context, too, many cases have been chronicled of people who seem to be magnets for apportation. Medium Herbert Baumann (1911-1998) is a striking example. For many years, author Illobrand von Ludwiger spent time with Baumann and reported more than one hundred instances of gems and crystals spontaneously appearing in his presence, often falling from above. In "Apport phenomena of medium Herbert Baumann Report on personal experiences," Ludwiger writes that, according to those personalities who spoke through Baumann in trance,

> the gems were apported from places where they were not missed or needed. They would be leftovers and Indeed, some of them show distinct signs of abrasion...as if they had been exposed to physical attrition, e.g., by lying in a riverbed for some time.

> Many of the stones apported [near] Baumann display peculiar networks of cracks and fissures that can reach such a density that [they have] become completely opaque. Sometimes, these cracks are concentrated in the center of the stones and don't reach the gem surface.

This reminds one of Barrie Colvin's analysis of spirit raps—that they originate deep *inside* the given substrate, rather than at the surface.

> When I showed gems with these "Baumann-cracks" to jewelers, they were not able to explain how they might have developed. They said that if a gem were to crack only once during the cutting process, they would normally stop cutting it because the stone would have become practically worthless, and would also be likely to break entirely.[44]

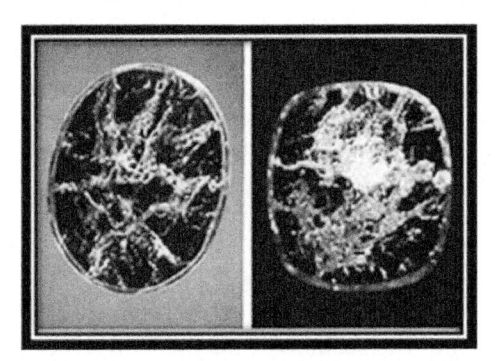

Two of hundreds of apported Baumann gems

It would stand to reason that, if such teleportation does involve disintegration at one location and reintegration at another, the latter process might not always go smoothly; even spirits can make mistakes, or else find a given situation lacking in the necessary vibratory conditions. In the same article, co-author Michael Nahm writes that other mediums, too, have experienced this same fragmentation of apports.

Similarly, in his book *Dei Fenomeni di "Apporto,"* Ernesto Bozzano presents numerous séance sessions in which the apported objects are described as having been disintegrated into minute particles at their site of origin and reassembled where they appear again.

> A well-known example was described by Bozzano (1930). On that occasion, he asked the disembodied spirit to bring a piece of pyrite from his [Bozzano's] home into the séance room. This attempt failed, but everything in the séance room was covered with a golden dust that seemed to be pyrite. When Bozzano returned home, he found that a notable piece of his pyrite chunk was missing.
>
> A similar incident was reported by Civitelli (1928). In this case, the sitters expected a silver thimble to be apported by [celebrated medium] Eusapia Palladino from a closed cupboard in another house, but the experiment failed. Still, when the owner of the thimble looked for it at home, all that she found on the spot where it had rested was a metallic powder that appeared to be silver.[45]

The apport phenomenon can stand as an object lesson, so to speak, representing all psychic/spiritual phenomena; in the quick transition away from an ordinary state of affairs, what we experience is not some new reality but a fresh reorganization of familiar reality—same ingredients, different recipe.

When an apported object arrives abruptly at its destination and regains its prior form, the force of this re-densification—the slamming back together—would be expected, even according to familiar physical laws, to produce kinetic energy. This could manifest as sound or heat, or both.

And this is indeed what we find. The first effect is reported by many, including members of the Scole Group and by von Ludwiger, who reports on two such episodes among many.

> In the evening, Baumann went into trance, lying on a couch in a darkened room. We three sat in a row of chairs about 2 meters in front of him. Suddenly, after

> Baumann had talked in trance for a while, we heard a sound like the crack of a whip about 1.5 to 2 meters behind us and at about 1 meter high, and then several pieces of something rolled toward us on the floor from behind.
>
> May 15, 1970, séance in Hamburg. On the audio recording, played at slow speed, one can clearly hear a loud bang. When we turned the light on, we found two pieces of an oblong crystal that was so full of cracks that it had become entirely opaque.[46]

The second predicted effect, heat, is also widely documented. "The apported stones were hot to the touch," von Ludwiger writes, "much hotter than body or air temperature."

> The origin of the Baumann-cracks might well be related to [this] unusual heat that the stones bore shortly after appearing—perhaps the heat being strongest in their center. I have personally felt this heat on several occasions, especially when I picked up larger stones right after they appeared. According to Baumann, his wife, and a friend, one particularly large, irregular crystal, 5 × 4 × 3 cm, appeared spontaneously under his shirt on his back when they were shopping in a large mall. Baumann was struck with pain and screamed, and, not knowing what was going on, supposing that perhaps a bird had flown into his clothes, they immediately tore his clothes off. Shop assistants and bystanders came running, and all were perplexed when suddenly this crystal was found...so hot that nobody could touch it, so Baumann wrapped it in a handkerchief and put it into a bag. A peculiar warmth of apported objects, especially of stones and metallic objects, has been reported before in the contexts of mediumship and poltergeist cases (e.g., Schwab 1923, Simsa 1934, Gauld & Cornell 1979, Hasted 1981, Zöllner 1922).[47]

The conscious intent behind apports is starkly evident whenever the objects are airmailed to appropriate recipients, as in the following examples.

4.8 Playful water and a wandering pig

Stewart Alexander, one of our great contemporary physical mediums, is still practicing today at eighty-three. Investigative journalist Leslie Kean is a member of his exclusive home circle. Compiling an impeccable forty-four-year track record, he has spent his adult life carrying the torch for those who have come before. I highly recommend "The Making of a Physical Medium" and "Experiences of a Physical Medium" on the New Thinking Allowed channel, and in his memoir *An Extraordinary Journey* (2010), Alexander shares many experiences that parallel and reaffirm phenomena produced decades and centuries earlier. Two are relevant here.

One night, a séance ended with no activity having taken place. When the lights were switched back on, the sitters' disappointment turned to astonishment.

> There, on the carpet, in front of every single member of the circle, was a little plastic animal about two inches in height—dogs, cats, sheep, etc.—a gift, no doubt, in recognition of each sitter's patience and dedication. Whilst everyone was understandably delighted by the apports, Kath had nothing in front of her. However, early the next morning, she called me in great excitement and told me the following story:

> When she retired to bed each evening, she was in the habit of reading. Then, when she began to feel tired, she would place her book on the bedside table and settle down. When she awoke that morning, the first thing she had seen, sitting on top of her book, was a pink plastic pig, about four inches in height—on the very book she herself had placed there only eight hours previously. She knew that her door had been securely locked and no one could have possibly been in her house during the night.[48]

Another time, long before the séance began, Alexander sat in the living room of Alan Crossley, another famous British physical medium. He noticed that

> a large vase filled with flowers and approximately a liter of water stood on a small table immediately in

front of a window. I noticed that every few moments, the blind, caught by the breeze, would rattle against the vase.

Alan was in the middle of relating one of his stories when, suddenly, the blind shot out and smashed into the vase, which tipped forward and fell towards the carpet. Alan ran into his kitchen and returned almost immediately, carrying a floor cloth. Getting down on his hands and knees and feeling the carpet, he stopped, rested back on his haunches, and began to laugh. "Come and see," he said. "Come and feel the carpet!" We realised that it was completely dry, and yet we had all clearly seen a large amount of water gush out of the vase moments earlier.

That evening, hours later, we were sitting in the circle in Alan's small séance room when little Christopher, our spirit communicator, calmly announced that he had something for us. There followed a whooshing sound, and in seconds we were all soaked to the skin by falling water. We were shocked, but after a few moments became highly amused. Somehow, the spirits had dematerialized the water from the vase in an instant, held it in suspension somewhere, and then, six hours later, returned it to us.[49]

At spirits' whim, a thing can be so flooded with IM that it doesn't just float…it vanishes. And then, the original ratio re-established later, the "missing" substance takes the stage again within our ordinary perceptual field; it was never missing after all or even "dematerialized"—just reconfigured.

Spirit playfulness seems designed to jostle us out of mortal dread, to clue us in to the simple range of fun to be had in a distance-free, fluid universe. The pink pig saga has a final twist.

> One day, Kath noticed with alarm that it was gone. A thorough search of the room, and then all of her other rooms, failed to unearth it.
>
> The weeks passed until a carpet fitter came to lay a new carpet in her lounge. The trumpet [common séance item] that we had used just the night before stood on her mantelpiece, and the fitter asked her if

she held séances here. When he was told yes, he immediately told her the following story, although he rather imagined that she would not believe him, because no one else did.

Several weeks earlier he had gone to bed and upon waking the following morning had seen, on his bedside table, a pink plastic pig. Kath then told him her own story, explaining that hers had suddenly disappeared several weeks earlier.

The two of them had never met or known of each other's existence. They lived eight miles apart. It just so happened that he, from amongst all his company's fitters, had been sent to lay Kath's carpet—weeks after finding the figure by his bed. She told him that her pink pig had a distinctive mark, and of course this identified it, so he returned it to her.[50]

British paranormal researcher Steve Mera shares a finding that speaks to the kinship between apports and UAPs. In "Tearing Down Walls Between UFO & Paranormal Studies" on the Steve Mera Official channel, he reports that

> A family in Morcom were having poltergeist-type disturbances, and they experienced an apported mug. The lady of the house went to get a cup of tea in the kitchen. She put the mug on the counter, put the kettle on, and when she turned back 'round, the mug was gone. She's looking all over for this mug; it never turns up until half an hour later. In the middle of the lounge carpet in the living area, right in the middle, you couldn't miss it, there was the mug.
>
> We asked if we could analyze it, and we took it to a university for atomic analysis. There was a diathermic [heat] reaction that had happened in that mug [subsequent to and different from the effects of the original firing in the kiln].
>
> Now, I knew I'd seen this diathermic reaction before. It was in an incident that took place where three people, independent witnesses, in vehicles, traveling down a road at night, suddenly saw this craft manifest near the

ground, in a field. The case was thoroughly investigated. The scientists found that the plants had been affected where this UFO was. They were stunted, they were wilted, didn't grow right. They decided to take samples and run "plant traumatology tests."

The diathermic reaction in the plants matched the diathermic reaction that we found in the apported mug. So, we might theorize that the manifestation of a UFO and the manifestation of an apported object are using the same physics.

4.9 The primordial synthesis

Astute readers will have felt a nagging question. If the elaborate, international dark matter particle detection projects have not yet registered an IM/OM interaction at the smallest scale—two of their elementary particles colliding to release a single-point burst of energy—either such interactions must be freakishly rare or else nonexistent. How, then, can I claim that macro-PK and other psychic/spiritual phenomena are due to the two matter types collaborating?

Because the nature of the case is fluid dynamics among fields, not IM and OM particles individually colliding. The synthesized, flowing system affects *itself*, internally orchestrated by consciousness. On the theoretical level of the MTR, IM and OM can be distinguished qualitatively, their shifting ratio invoked, but in practice they are integrated—David Bohm's "single undivided whole."

Physicists, I predict, will never "discover" IM directly—beyond its indirect gravitational effect—but if they should turn their attention to psychic/spiritual phenomena, they could easily identify it albeit still indirectly, by inference, by process of elimination. In Appendix K, I suggest a few experiments for testing the MTR—the matter-type ratio theory.

If IM and OM each contribute about 50% of the mass of reality, you might wonder why, when we weigh things, even air, they don't come out to twice what we'd expect? This is because the primordial synthesis of matter types is already baked into our expectations, though we're unaware of it. The invisible contribution cannot be factored in until we recognize that massive blind spot. Since the beginning, OM has never existed independently; *there is no such thing as OM without IM*.

Like all fundamental fields (see sections 2.2 and 2.3), the fundamental consciousness field is not a substance in itself; rather, it *produces* substance (particles of IM) through "excitations" of energy, and there is no theoretical limit on this production. In other words, the level of IM in a given space can proliferate to the extent that further energy is introduced. What is the source of this energy? Conscious intent. You are making some IM right now just by reading these words. Those adept at macro-PK spawn and direct a lot of it when willing a table to levitate. Certain spirits can focus themselves enough to affect the ordinary physical world by the same means.

But how can IM, the least-dense, highest-frequency substance in existence, create density? Haven't I argued that IM *reduces* density in the microclimate of a room when spirits pay a visit? The reason is that the fundamental consciousness field can work in both directions, modulating the frequencies involved, rarefying OM when breezing through a room or making a table buoyant, compacting it slightly—by withdrawing itself to a degree—in order to render a séance table suddenly too heavy to lift, to re-densify an apported gemstone, or to make a UAP flash into view.

Besides adjusting the density of existing OM objects, IM can create *new* objects as well. That materializing spirit, re-entering Earth's vibrational environment, has plenty of ambient OM raw material at its disposal to draw from; see Appendix E.

As we've learned, this is true on the largest scale too: IM brings order to cosmological raw materials—the wandering fog of hot gas and dust—condensing them into stars with solar systems, and then sculpting these into sprawling spiral galaxies.

Both primordially and proximally, then, the IM/OM alchemy governs the very stuff of reality.

Chapter 5
The Dance of Density
Shrinking the "Problem Space" of UAPs and Spirits

In each case the so-called spacecraft did not disappear by moving away, even at high speed. It simply vanished on the spot, or it slowly faded aay like the Cheshire cat, sometimes leaving behind a whitish cloud. In other cases, UFOs have been reported to enter the ground.
— Jacques Vallée, *Dimensions: A Casebook of Alien Contact*

Sometimes the abductees will experience their own bodies as if they were filled with light or simply were light. The vibration may be quite intense, as if to fill all the experiencers' cells, which feel as if they are separating from each other or coming apart at the "molecular" level.
—John E. Mack, *Passport to the Cosmos*

We typically assume [the visitors'] travel must involve arcane cosmological machinery such as a wormhole or "stargate." But I became increasingly drawn to the idea that our visitors' method of travel is less flashy (from a technical perspective) and more understandable in terms of Earthly paranormal influences. This form of travel might be accomplished without the need for energy-intensive machinery; if shamanic experiences are any indication, the ability to transcend space and time might be a more fitting subject for parapsychologists than for theoretical physicists.
—Mac Tonnies, *The Cryptoterrestrials*

overview

- Shrinking our "problem space" (the parameters of an inquiry) with respect to UAPs and psychic/spiritual reality, we can more tightly frame these kindred

subjects, demystifying them to some extent in preparation for more efficient progress going forward.
- We discuss phenomena and conscious agents that exist on higher vibrational levels than us.
- We assess the mutual resonance among an array of paranormal phenomena, establish consciousness as the prime mover behind them all, and consider the promise of "metamaterials."

5.1 Seeing one level deeper

It will appear that they have suddenly arrived in your skies in great number. In reality this is untrue. For in reality they are where they have always been, but man sees with new eyes.
—John Keel, *Operation Trojan Horse*

Density is the crux of the matter, which is the same as saying that frequency is the crux of the matter; as we've seen, frequency is inversely proportional to density: The lower the frequency of something, the higher its density, and vice versa.

Fluctuations of frequency are perpetually bubbling just behind the scenes. While most of us see air in clear weather as invisible, some are able to perceive a much more "involved" medium right before their eyes. "Space that was empty never existed for me," wrote celebrated Irish medium Eileen Garrett (1893-1970) in *My Life as a Search for the Meaning of Mediumship*.

I first became aware of movement in light and colour before I was five years old. I grew conscious of it by lying still on my bed and looking into the shadows. I began then to see globules of light bursting at intervals within the beams of sunlight. When I knew them better, I discovered them moving in any kind of light; they swirled around each other, enlarging and bursting as bubbles do, when they give way one to the other; and just as bubbles reflect colour, so also did the bursting globules have colour within them. These light balls presented themselves in so many shapes and sizes that my head ached from trying to see them all moving simultaneously in many directions.[51]

No one else in Garrett's life, especially her young classmates, could see what she saw, and so she had "to learn to live in two worlds." It's as though she was wearing special glasses that allowed her to watch matter-type collaborations, driven by consciousness, that fall outside the range of typical human vision.

During a long and fruitful career, Garrett became a world-renowned medium, conveying to thousands information from departed loved ones, whose spirits she could often see. Throughout history, people like her have been aware of spirits all around them, in endless forms, moods, and moral states, because they're able to tune in to higher vibrations than most. Though such clairvoyants were often persecuted, killed, or ostracized from society, their gift was anything but supernatural. It's entirely natural to resonate spirit to spirit within the fundamental consciousness field; while still living on Earth, the old saying goes, "We are just as much spirit now as we ever shall be."

Fast forward a century and a quarter, and now we possess technology—digital photography—that opens a surprising window onto the same "globules of light" that four-year-old Eileen Garrett beheld. In *The Orb Project* (2007), Klaus Heinemann and Micheál Ledwith analyze the phenomenon from various angles and debunk efforts to explain all orbs away as mere photographic artifacts, such as "backscatter" from unfocused motes of dust, which can be easily differentiated from genuine orbs both visually and in terms of behavior. Genuine orbs do not drift about aimlessly but rather move with clear intent and intelligence. They often "survey" an onlooker or group, traveling in a circle or semi-circle, or "patrol" an area in a grid pattern. Also, they will occasionally respond to an onlooker's thoughts, rising when she thinks "go up," etc.

"Orbs and the realms they inhabit are fundamentally not a matter of faith but of physics," write the authors of *The Orb Project*.

It's the first time that we have encountered the paranormal in a readily accessible form, easily available for observation by anyone on a regular basis.

Human vision operates only within a narrow band. Knowing this, it is actually comical how readily anything that falls outside it is dismissed as unreal. We tend to see *this* world as real, and everything else is just levels of "frequencies." These frequencies are actually realms that are just as substantial as this "physical" one. The realms of existence we used to call "beyond"...are now less mysterious.[52]

I find this partial demystification helpful. We can't hope to fully comprehend such manifestations before we ourselves transition, but to gain a little traction on the spiritual mode of existence is quite a mental windfall. It resonates with so many near-death experiencers' descriptions of being transformed—or restored—into "a sphere of pure awareness" that is their natural condition. Numerous closely matching testimonials can be found in books and on YouTube. Dr. Peter Cummings's near-death experience: "I was able to see everything around me, 360 degrees." Deborah King's NDE: "I could take in information in 360 degrees, not in the linear way anymore."

Whitley Strieber, of *Communion* fame, has been apparently lucky enough to communicate with his wife Annie, who transitioned in 2015. "The soul can be detected," she's assured him, echoing the general consensus. "Those orbs that people record...those are souls moving slow enough to be seen"—slow enough in velocity and low enough in vibration.

As with orbs, exactly so with human spirits manifesting in other forms. In *Surviving Death*, Leslie Kean relays an analogy offered by physical medium Stewart Alexander, whom we met in section 4.8.

> Stewart told me that the spirit people exist in an etheric body at a higher vibration. It's like taking a bamboo pole and swinging it so fast the eye can't see it anymore. The pole is still there, but it's moving too fast, vibrating too rapidly.... The spirit people have to slow themselves down...when they materialize.[53]

Hummingbirds or dragonflies, too, for that matter, operate near the edge of our perception; if they flew just seven times faster, we'd never see them unless they hovered or landed, at which point they'd seem to appear out of thin air. Of course, spiritual invisibility isn't typically a matter of velocity on the macro scale; it's velocity on the micro scale—high vibration *within* the entity in question. But the mere fact that we can find rough parallels with terrestrial creatures reduces the "boggle factor," shrinks the problem space of our effort to understand what beings of various densities are like.

"The Spiritualistic Séance"

5.2 Orbs and UAPs

They are like two peas in a pod, in terms of both behavior and mutual proximity.

- *Behavior*. Like orbs, UAPs become visible only when they deliberately slow down in velocity and vibration. On his fascinating YouTube channel Custodian File, for example, Dr. Robert Shiepe films helicopters, planes, parasails, balloons, blimps, etc., from his Marina del Rey, CA, balcony. Why? Six years ago, he caught unexpected glimpses and finally realized that anything in the air above 150 feet was being consistently "tagged" (passed at close range) by miniature UAPs traveling at incredible speeds. He calls them "dragons" because initially, he thought they must be nearby dragonflies until, with two cameras, he was able to triangulate on the position of one and fix its distance at 1734 feet. He's also been able to estimate the objects' average velocity at 2000 miles per hour, which means that they are not visible until he slows the footage way, way down, often to just 3% original speed. From all over the world now, people are now sending him videos that capture the very same procedure—at air shows, airports, etc.—which he's also sharing on his channel. Shiepe aims to spread awareness of the predictability and ubiquity of these tiny monitors so that they can be integrated into our understanding of the broader UAP enigma.

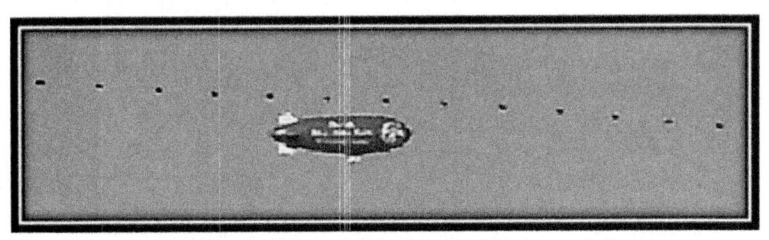

Frame-by-frame stills of a "dragon" buzzing a blimp; each frame represents 1/60th of a second, so the UAP is many times faster than any bird.

See also "Dr. Brown: Pushing UFO Disclosure with New Photography" on the Chris Lehto channel. Courtney Brown is teaching a photographic method that can capture UAPs moving at 15,000 to 20,000 miles per hour and visible only in the infrared spectrum at 120 frames per second. He contends that any twenty-minute daytime video of the sky over an urban area, using this method will reveal numerous UAP, fully unsuspected by the citizens below. He shows examples very reminiscent of Shiepe's "dragons," including one in which the UAP zips along, making a nearby jet— going 400-500 mpg—appear to be standing still. Foreground insects are ruled out because the camera is focused at infinity: anything close is extremely blurry.

- *Mutual proximity.* The more UAP encounters you learn about, the more you'll notice orbs/spheres popping up. Some are apparently metallic, unlike spirit orbs, while others—balls of energy—do match spiritual description. This is not to say that the two types spring from the same source, though they occasionally might; nonetheless, their kinship is striking. A large craft is often seen flanked or followed by glowing orbs, or it will release them. When UAPs are hovering above, orbs tend to manifest near the ground, close at hand—as though "scouting" the location and the witness(es).

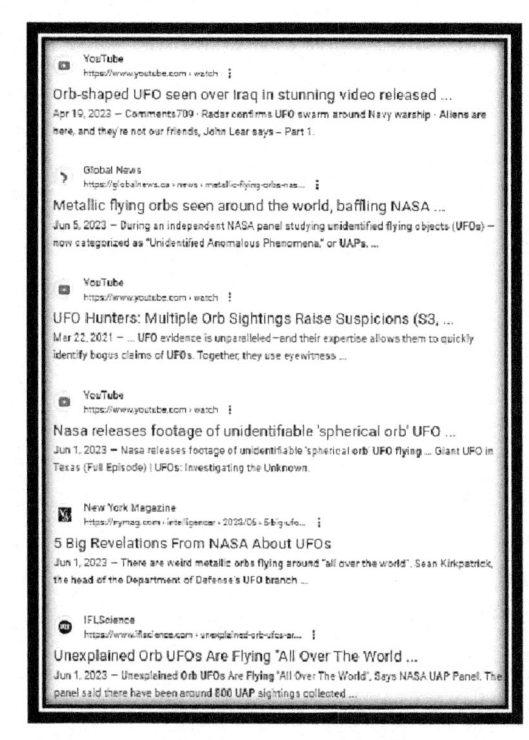

An object in the process of materializing—gaining density—would want to do so in the most energetically cost-effective manner. A sphere is an extremely efficient design, possessing the lowest possible surface-area-to-volume ratio and therefore requiring the least energy to establish and maintain; hence, natural objects like bubbles and raindrops, planets and suns assume this shape. This, the relative ease, is probably also why spirits favor this form when undertaking a return to Earth's frequency range.

Of course, UAPs come in a striking variety of other configurations, too, many far from aerodynamic; this further testifies to their immunity to friction and drag. In 2020, for instance, a cube-shaped object was caught on video at 30,000 feet by a commercial pilot over Medellin,

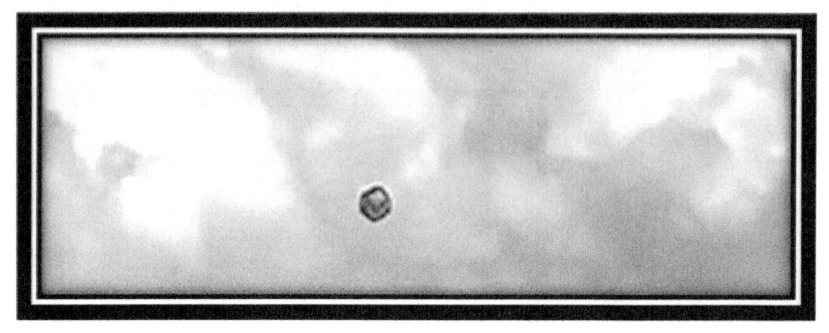

Columbia; see "Cube-Shaped UFO Shocks Pilot" on the History Channel's YouTube channel.

5.3 A clear MTR example from Skinwalker Ranch

Skinwalker Ranch is a property in northeastern Utah with a deep history of UAPs and other paranormal activity. I recommend the History Channel series "The Secret of Skinwalker Ranch," in which a team of investigators chronicles frequent UAP appearances, atmospheric aberrations, and other "high strangeness." In Season 4, Episode 11, the team deploys a LiDAR system onto a spot where a preponderance of anomalies has occurred. LiDar (light detection and ranging) uses laser beams to "see" the world in 3D, providing computers an accurate representation of the surveyed environment; like radar and sonar, it registers the amount of time its signals take to bounce back. Travis Taylor and the others are stunned to find a void with sharply defined edges. The black is where all the light has been absorbed, creating a "data sink" containing zero information. The team immediately leaps to "portal," "black hole" or "wormhole." The MTR theory would instead interpret this effect as simply a local concentration, a spiked IM/OM ratio such that the composition becomes invisible; as we know, IM won't reflect light. No "hole" needed, worm or otherwise. Though the image does not contain temperature information, I would wager that the air in the black spot was cold.

5.4 Temperature and MTR

> On their first night at Skinwalker Ranch, Admiral Axelrod and two colleagues took a walk on the dark land. After about half a mile, "the temperature suddenly dropped like a stone. From 75 degrees, the air was now 20 degrees colder. All three walked backwards and within a couple of yards, the temperature had gone back to the mid-70s. The three moved silently in unison. Again, they walked into a wall of cold."[54]

You'll recall that in the previous chapter, I offered my best explanation for why psychic/spiritual events are often associated with cold spots and cold breezes; see section 4.6. With the intentional gathering of low-density consciousness, IM proliferates in a given place, producing a microclimate shift. The IM/OM ratio spikes and the barometric pressure falls slightly, resulting in a noticeable temperature drop and a brief displacement of OM air, felt as a breeze.

The UAP enigma, too, involves such effects. David Mason, featured in the documentary "A Tear in the Sky," has filmed UAPs that frustrate all conventional models of propulsion. The energy demands involved in keeping a large object aloft and traveling at thousands of miles per hour ought to create extreme heat. Furthermore, if the object is just arriving from space, we would expect it to have built up tremendous heat while entering our atmosphere. On the contrary, however, Mason explains that, by using thermal cameras, he has taken the temperature of high-flying craft that "register at minus 20 Fahrenheit. I've even had some down to minus 80, which is just extraordinarily cold. *And they exhibit no exhaust.*"[55] For additional such data, see Appendix F.

Likewise, the famous "GoFast" UAP, filmed by the US Navy in 2015, was not hot. NASA's 2023 "UAP Independent Study Team Report" even attempts to debunk it on these grounds.

> The object appears bright against a dark ocean. For these display settings, this indicates that the object is colder than the ocean. There is thus no evidence of heat produced by a propulsion system. This supports the conjecture that the object is most likely just drifting with the wind.[56]

NASA apparently can't conceive of a means of rapid transport that does not generate heat. By the same token, I'm sure they'd guffaw at the mere suggestion of macro-PK such as levitation and apportation, though they can offer no viable alternative.

UAPs are not always cold. Some, such as the "gimbal" object, register as hot, while others toggle back and forth. But if they can *ever* operate while cold, this means that their modus operandi lies beyond consensus aeronautics and known physics writ large.

Witnesses have reported UAPs appearing and disappearing in quick succession along their trajectory, "skipping like a stone across a pond." Many interpret this behavior as proof positive that the vehicles are "interdimensional." I see it as nothing more exotic than the malleability of matter, well known for centuries within psychic/spiritual research. The craft are akin to séance apports, but unlike apports, they never arrive for good (unless they crash or are shot down); they're in continual strobic oscillation between density modes such that they are never solid objects in the ordinary sense, unless they land, and then only briefly. This dance on the boundary is what allows for the fluid shapeshifting so often described, and for the so-called "cloaking" of UAPs, a misnomer.

Physicists' best guess thus far for "how they do it" is the "warp drive," which I described in section 1.2. However, if this gravity-bending technology were ever practically realized—as in the systems proposed by Salvatore Pais or Jack Sarfatti—it would require a massive amount of energy to operate, and this, according to the first law of thermodynamics (the conservation of energy), would necessarily convert into extreme heat.

You may be wondering why apported gems tend to arrive piping hot, as documented for example in the Herbert Baumann case (section 4.7), whereas UAPs are frequently cold. I think it's because, in the former case, the object is regaining density all at once, slamming together, which produces kinetic energy/heat and often a loud sound as well. UAPs, on the other hand, though they do transition from invisible to visible as they enter our frequency range, are still of low density when they first appear, allowing us to track them and take their temperature; they're poised in that liminal space between modes, effectively—from our limited perspective—*both there and not there*. This low-density condition is what keeps their temperature low in contrast to their surroundings. It's also what permits them to escape the effects of friction/drag, pass from air to water without losing velocity, and even occasionally to sink into solid ground.

The eerie silence of UAPs is one of their hallmarks. Occasionally, however, sightings are associated with acoustics akin to those of the apport phenomenon. You'll recall that the Baumann crystals produced sound upon arrival: "On the audio recording…one can clearly hear a loud bang. When we turned the light on, we found two pieces of an oblong crystal." In "UFO Sightings and Loud Booms" on Cristina Gomez's channel, she shares a well-documented case.

> On April 16, 2008, residents of Kokomo, Indiana, experienced an unusual event characterized by bright flashes in the sky followed by "a huge, thundering boom," much stronger than any sonic boom, which caused physical vibrations in the area…[with] structural shaking, activation of car alarms, and widespread concern among the community. No earthquake was detected by seismologists.

I would presume that this effect is produced by a particularly abrupt density transition from lower to higher. See also "Flashing Light and Thundering Boom in Minnesota Mystify Federal Officials" on the Quirk Zone channel.

5.5 Clustering and the hitchhiker effect

> *An understanding of the nature of the UFO phenomenon could provide new insights into unusual events that have not yet been duplicated in the laboratory. It would give a clue to the mechanism of some psychic processes. Phenomena of precognition, telepathy, and even healing are not unusual among the reports, especially when they involve close-range observation of an object or direct exposure to its light.*
> —John Mack, *Abduction*

> *They are constructed both as physical craft and as psychic devices whose exact properties remain to be defined. In the last twenty-five years, at least ten thousand sightings of unidentified flying objects have been filed away unexplained by competent investigators...but no bridge has yet been built between this body of data and the evidence that exists for psychic phenomena such as precognition, psychokinesis, and telepathy.*
> —Jacques Vallée, *Dimensions*

On June 24, 1947, a month prior to the notorious Roswell event, Kenneth Arnold—the man who coined the term "saucers" to describe the vehicles—saw nine UAPs over Mount Ranier in Washington State. Long after he died, Arnold's daughter publicly disclosed "that she'd seen orbs in their house after his sighting. She also experienced various poltergeist effects."[57]

The so-called *hitchhiker effect* refers to psychic/spiritual phenomena that begin after, and are apparently triggered by, UAP encounters; the chain reaction "follows a person home." The best-known instances have involved visitors to Skinwalker Ranch. In addition to playing host to high-velocity UAPs streaking across its skies both day and night, the site also manifests episodes identical to psychic events reported worldwide—but clustered here and uncannily consistent. Indeed, most of the ground-level drama associated with the Ranch closely mirrors what has been well known in Spiritualist circles since the first successful séances in Hydesville, New York, in 1849.

And their sharing space with UAPs is, of course, particularly relevant to our main theme.

As chronicled in *Skinwalkers at the Pentagon*, the hitchhiker effect was particularly intense in the case of Jonathan Axelrod, a two-star admiral within Naval Intelligence with Top Secret/Sensitive Compartmented Information clearances. After his visit to the Ranch in July 2009, during which he experienced a range of paranormal episodes, he returned home, whereupon

> every member of his family experienced orbs in their house two thousand miles away, saw dark humanoid creatures in their bedrooms, and heard multiple sounds of footsteps at night. The teenagers endured harrowing episodes in their bedrooms. Paul, the younger teenager, claims to have been attacked by blue and red orbs in his bedroom on the night of February 7, 2011. One day, they found their dog up on the roof.[58]

Nor were the anomalies limited to the family; they began to spread within the neighborhood.

> Paul was approached by one of his high school friends, who told him that on the previous night, he had looked out his bedroom window and had witnessed a large wolf-like creature standing outside, looking in at him. A few weeks later, another friend told Paul of seeing strange blue lights flying around his backyard. These revelations by the two friends came without prompting from Paul. In other words, they cannot be dismissed as "me too" phenomena. The experiences suggest that the perception of bizarre creatures and blue orbs was transferable beyond the Axelrod family home.[59]

A military intelligence agent named Witt visited the Ranch and then, when she returned home, she too entered the uncanny fray, having never experienced such things before.

> She reported hearing loud banging sounds from her kitchen and heavy footsteps on her stairs. The poltergeist activity escalated in Witt's townhouse, and on one occasion both she and her roommate were in the living room when two wine bottles suddenly flew off the rack, hurtled across the room in front of them,

and smashed loudly and messily on the opposite wall. She said she frequently awoke to find black shadow-like figures in her room near her bed and observed different-colored orbs. Her fiancé eventually moved out, and several years later, Witt was still experiencing the poltergeist-like activity.[60]

The uncanny contagion is reliably reproducible. In the current research era under Ranch owner Brandon Fugal, cast members of the History Channel program witness, during production hiatuses, the same breakouts back home.

As mentioned, though, the effect is by no means limited to this one situation. "People who have never been on Skinwalker Ranch and just interact with the UAP phenomenon," says Colm Kelleher, "report elements of the hitchhiker effect, in cases where we have the luxury of being able to study them over many months or many years."[61] And Jacques Vallée speaks of the new sensitivities and PK gifts that UAPs tend to leave in their wake, post-encounter effects such as "coincidences of a telepathic nature. Clocks and electrical circuits have been affected…and a doctor has experienced levitation without being able to control it."[62]

Significantly, the same expansion of one's psychic/spiritual reality frame is also found in people following near-death experiences; see *The Omega Project: Near-Death Experiences, UFO Encounters, and Mind at Large* by Kenneth Ring and Bruce Greyson, "Increase in psychic phenomena following near-death experiences" by Bruce Greyson, and "Psychic Phenomena Following Near-Death Experiences: An Australian Study" by Cherie Sutherland.

So, what's the take-away from all of this viral clustering?

5.6 The kinship key

Everything is vibration.
—Albert Einstein

If you want to find the secrets of the universe, think in terms of frequency and vibration.
—Nikola Tesla

Resonance occurs when a vibrating object causes another nearby object to vibrate at a higher frequency.

Imagine a steel ball on a string. If you give it a push, it will start to swing back and forth. If you push it again and again in the same direction, it will speed up every time *because you're adding energy to the system.* Or picture a wine glass under the influence of an opera singer's high note; if the note matches the natural frequency of the glass, it will automatically raise that frequency until it shatters.

I think this helps to explain the hitchhiker effect and clustering. If you once come into contact with a conscious psychic/spiritual agent, you are then more prone to resonate with others because, in the initial instance, the agent had to lower its frequency to meet you where you live, to resonate with you. This raised your own frequency during the encounter, conditioning you to further such connections, because instead of shattering like the wine glass, you gained a new energy signature or resident frequency.

Recalling Barrie G. Colvin's finding (in section 4.5) that poltergeist "raps" result from a build-up of pressure within the structure of tables or walls, we may surmise that the agents in question are intentionally resonating with the natural frequency of the wood, thus adding energy and causing small explosions analogous to what happens to the wine glass.

I often ask myself this question: Just because psychic/spiritual phenomena emerge from a larger reality frame, does this necessarily mean that 1. this is always the *same* larger reality frame, or that 2. the phenomena need have anything in common? Then, I remember my guiding premise: There exist two and only two fundamental matter types, and the invisible type represents the fundamental consciousness field, operating at much higher frequencies. Therefore, whatever comes to our attention from outside the narrow range of OM experience must be due to IM's influence on OM. There can't be multiple "outsides" because, as shown in Chapter 3, *the fundamental consciousness field is one continuous reality*—though the array of frequencies and conscious agents operating therein seems to be vast.

Psychic/spiritual phenomena breaking into our experience are not merely similar to one another, they are also vibrational neighbors and *mutually resonant* (hence, clustering); that is, their shared association with certain people and events does not resemble some random collection of episodes. The kinship between, say, table levitation and

UAP levitation, or between person-to-person telepathy and visitor-to-person telepathy, or between a human spirit's ability to pass through walls and a UAP's immunity to hurricane-force gales, or between the appearance/disappearance of apports and the appearance/disappearance of UAPs, is far from superficial.

5.7 The UAP propulsion system is consciousness

The little ones, they were just flowing around in the air. They didn't touch the ground.
—Ariel School UAP landing witness, Zimbabwe, 1994

Cases of uncontrolled levitation or gravity effects have been reported in connection with UFOs. In one case, which took place in 1954 in the French countryside, a man who was coming back from the fields with his horse had to let go of the bridle as the animal was lifted several feet into the air—a dark, circular object was flying fast over the trail they were following.
—Jacques Vallée

I've been told that a large part of what's been frustrating our attempts to reverse-engineer this technology is the shortage of people who have the capacity to consciously engage with it. You need a particular type of person to operate it, using your mind.
—Ross Coulthart, author of *In Plain Sight*

Researcher and documentarian Jeremy Corbell says, "My understanding is that we have not been able to duplicate the core UAP technologies." In the same vein, Lue Elizondo ponders his "five observables."

It turns out that a lot of the maneuvers we've seen—instantaneous acceleration, unparalleled velocities, low observability, trans-medium travel, and of course positive lift or anti-gravity—for many years we tried to figure out separately, each from the perspective of some sort of exotic technology. One of our findings was that it may very well be that all of those observables are actually a manifestation of a single technology: If you know how to do X, all these other things can now occur."[63]

What is this "core," this "X," the holy grail of UAP performance? We've spent untold billions trying to master the technology by means of small-m materialism. It's time to expand the circle to reach a much more fruitful perspective—the capital-M Materialism that embraces all matter at all densities/frequencies.

Many UAP experiencers describe a craft just hovering in the air, making no noise, expending no obvious energy. The humanoid occupants, too, often seem unencumbered by gravity, yet you don't find physicists seeking to understand the Grays' individual "propulsion systems." Rather than warping spacetime to create a gravitationally isolated envelope or bubble, craft and crew have simply taken gravity out of the equation entirely. Witnesses don't perceive them as occupying a separate pocket of spacetime any more than members of a séance group see levitating tables that way.

It seems that our visitors have reached a level of proficiency in intention-driven macro-PK that we earthlings—*and even our spirit counterparts*—can still only dabble in as rank amateurs. But don't forget the always-helpful distinction between kind and degree. Even floating a pencil one inch off the desktop, mere child's play in the big picture, is proof of concept, no different in *kind* but only in *degree* from the most spectacular aerial displays.

It further seems that our visitors possess a collective *hive mind* far more integral, cohesive, and pragmatic than our own spiritual "oneness"; perhaps they are not even individuals at all in any meaningful sense. Lifting and controlling OM objects—craft sometimes the size of football fields—is evidently well within the capacity of their psychic solidarity.

If it's true that UAPs are operated by group consciousness, then we can say with confidence that their energy category is not electromagnetic (see Appendix C), a claim backed up by their thermodynamic neutrality. What to make, then, of the very common accounts of our electronics being tangled with and disabled in their presence? What of the bright lights on the ships and the beams witnesses see? Well, the fundamental consciousness field is distinct from the fields that underlie other aspects of nature, but all fields can interact; see section 2.3. As in typical cases of psychic/spiritual activity, electrons are often engaged by UAPs and their occupants; that is, they can evidently produce electromagnetic effects—consciousness influences OM in many ways, as we've seen—even though that field is not the *source* of their power.

In an interview, renowned theoretical physicist Jack Sarfatti shares what he's learned through a reliable source: "Every detail about the object described by Colonel Philip Corso in *The Day After Roswell* is accurate."

> The "saucer" was about 30-35 feet in diameter, weighed about a ton and a half, 3000 pounds, and inside it's almost empty. There's no obvious propulsion mechanism. There's just three small seats for the Grays, and they control the ship with their brainwaves. I can confirm all that is true, crazy as it sounds.[64]

From thousands of encounter reports, we can gather that these Grays seem to be the frontmen, mere worker drones or biological robots, dutifully executing their roles for superiors. As such, they are part and parcel of the vast swarm that's running the macro-PK show.

5.8 Metamaterials as arrows to the future

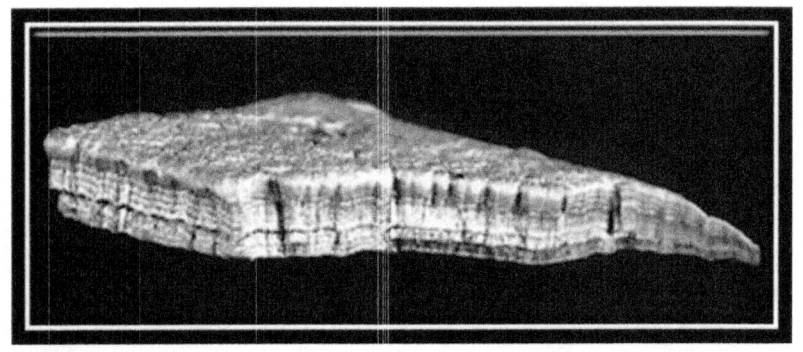

Metal "skin" retrieved from the bottom of a "wedge-shaped craft" in 1948 west of Sierra Blanca Mountain on White Sands Missile Range, composed of 36 layers alternating: 1-4 microns pure black bismuth with 100-200 microns magnesium (97.6%) and zinc alloy (2.4%). Each of the pieces from the US Army source was "formed" with a tapered curvature.

Alongside the high-stakes search for propulsion technology, with its geopolitical military implications, an equally charged pursuit has centered on *metamaterials*. A metamaterial is any material engineered to have a property that is rarely or never observed in naturally occurring materials. They are made from assemblies of multiple elements fashioned from composite materials, typically metals. In *UAP Propulsion: A Metamaterial Approach to Spacetime Control*, Jon Plus writes,

> Metamaterials give us new ways to exquisitely sculpt electromagnetic effects. Spacetime itself may not lie far removed from the electromagnetic domain.
> The canvas is vast and the medium speculative, but insights can emerge when colors mix together into new shades. The artist does not know the final image but progresses stroke by stroke. By precisely controlling fundamental electromagnetic phenomena, we enhance our influence over resulting fields and forces. Metamaterials offer a versatile toolkit to deliberately manipulate electromagnetic phenomena in ways no natural material can match. By dynamically tuning the metamaterial, spacetime distortions [might] move and morph as needed for propulsive functions.[65]

You see the problem here: It's all electromagnetism all the time. And this is why, by all accounts, scientists remain stymied by UAP "magic"; they're barking up the wrong tree.

Interviewed on ex-Navy pilot and UAP eyewitness Ryan Graves' podcast, Stanford professor Garry Nolan reports that "The word on the street is that nobody understands how these things operate. They don't know where the battery is. They don't know where the engine is." But since he is a materials scientist, rather than letting this strange observation lead him beyond a reductive small-m materialism, Nolan assumes that "somehow, they [battery and engine] are embedded in the structure of the craft."

So, why even feature metamaterials here at all if their pursuit is short-sighted? Because while I doubt that working in this arena will allow us to solve the UAP propulsion riddle, I do think that analyzing the composition of the materials the visitors themselves use may ultimately send us down a fruitful path.

Pieces of metal alleged to have come from UAPs under well-documented circumstances—see Jacques Vallée's study "What do we Know about the Material Composition of UFOs?"—have been analyzed using *mass spectrometers* and their makeup found to be different from metals occurring naturally; therefore, it seems, they must have been manufactured. One of the samples Nolan analyzed, for example, "contained magnesium ratios that were so far off from what you'd dig out of the ground that it must have been engineered in some industrial process."[66]

However, he points out that this technology is still quite limited; it can only detect ratios of elements and compounds, whereas we need to understand the material *atom by atom*.

> The granularity that we require to understand these things is not there. We need to know where the atoms are in 3D space in order to get at the bond structure of the objects. The level of detail we need to reach and exploit would involve isotopes [subtle variations] of elements. Humans currently paint the world in 85 elements, whereas we could be painting the world—and maybe somebody else already *is*—in the 253 stable isotopes. They're in technicolor, we're still in black and white.[67]

And here lies the reason to study metamaterials. In building their craft out of OM constituents according to certain exacting rules that we can't yet understand, the visitors are presumably maximizing the vibrational fluency or elasticity of their metals. That is, these objects must be able to transition to and fro across IM/OM ratios, and an ideal constellation of atoms must exist.

The kindred phenomenon of apports demonstrates that many different kinds of objects are susceptible to such conscious teleportation, but we find that a certain class of object represents the vast majority of apports across the centuries. As we saw in the remarkable case of Herbert Baumann (section 4.8), crystals and gems can readily appear, and it turns out that they dominate the apport picture generally. What is it about them that lends itself to such transmissibility? The obvious property is their extremely high natural frequency band, which puts them closer already to the IM register from the get-go. As we know, every substance possesses a unique vibrational signature, and a pure crystalline solid is way up there among materials because of its fixed, regularly repeating, perfect geometric pattern known as a *crystal lattice*.

Significantly, metals recovered from UAPs also possess "an unusually pure, crystalline structure,"[68] according to Nolan. It is to be hoped that further probing will eventually unlock UAP metamaterial qualities and potentials that point us beyond the bland OM paradigm—to the vivid and versatile "technicolor" of the mind.

Preliminary breakthroughs may even be afoot already. DC Long describes gaining access to a subterranean hangar and being shocked to observe massive levitating objects: "DC Long—Army Combat Vet's Mysterious UFO Encounter in Underground Military Base" on the Shawn Ryan Show. Note that Long emphasizes an intense vibration associated with the objects—likely a frequency-raising resonance.

5.9 BREAKING: the P3 program

> *I asked an insider, "What was the first thought that went through your mind when you learned about the P3 program?" He answered that it confirmed that there is an afterlife.*
> —Michael Herrera

Though I had good reason to believe, on theoretical grounds, that the UAP propulsion system is, at bottom, driven by consciousness, it wasn't until October of 2023 that I heard the first public hint of confirmation. This is when Ross Coulthart shared his scoop that "A large part of what's been frustrating our attempts to reverse-engineer this technology is the shortage of people who have the capacity to consciously engage with it."

And then, just a month later, I heard former US Marine Michael Herrera share concrete details of a program, already seventy-six years old, to integrate consciousness directly into the reverse-engineering effort. On former USAF fighter pilot Chris Lehto's podcast, Herrera explained that, back in 1947, after Roswell and two other such incidents of downed UAPs, President Truman's signing of the National Security Act had retasked the robust and hermetically sealed infrastructure of the Manhattan Project to the study of nonhuman intelligences, NIH.

Having no idea, though, how the recovered craft actually *worked*, authorities soon realized that

> there was a mismatch, a missing link. When they finally figured out that people possessing higher consciousness existed on Earth that could [step in to fill the gap], that's basically how they solved the problem.

One day, the ins and outs of this realization process will make for a stunning exposé.

According to Herrera, thousands of psychically gifted individuals have been "scooped up," across the years and across the planet, for the Psionic Predisposition Potential (P3) Program and installed as go-betweens—or mediums, if you will. Psionics is a word straight out of science fiction of the 50s and 60s, meaning the application of principles of engineering to the study and implementation of paranormal or psychic phenomena, such as extrasensory perception, telepathy, and psychokinesis (PK).

The worldwide recruits have been extracted predominantly from developing countries and the Native American population—*along with their families*. They are not held against their will. They understand that they're better off now, according to Herrera. The reasoning is that

> if they take someone who's not used to the lifestyle of being a P3 asset, where you have everything provided for you and your family, medical, housing, food, clean water, your children getting free educations, then they are unlikely to want to leave or leak information. It's heaven compared to where they were at before. It's like any business exploiting poor societies for a cheap labor force.[70]

At this point, while the nuances of the P3 program operations remain shrouded in secrecy, the shroud is beginning to fray. Herrera claims to have learned that widespread blood screening has been used to identify genetic markers for a certain brain anomaly associated with psychic giftedness. In about one out of every 250 people, this anomaly confers a greater abundance, an "over-expression," of neurons. Often called "the brain within the brain," the *caudate-putamen* region is involved in one's movement through the world and in intuitive information processing, especially involving subtle patterns. "If intuition is the ability to see things in front of you that other people might just dismiss," says Garry Nolan, then it would lend itself to the perception of UAPs.

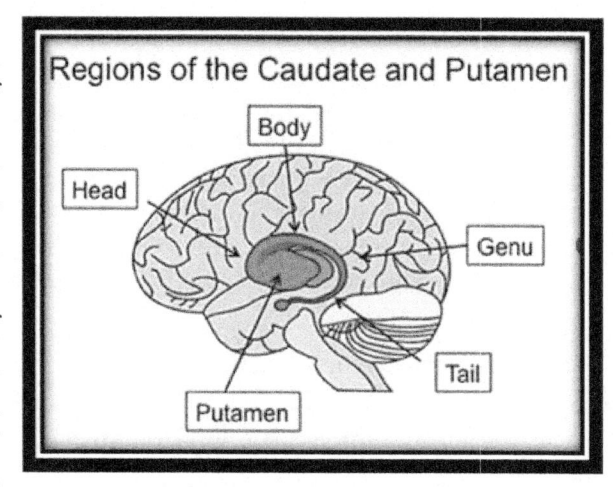

In 2020, Nolan undertook an fMRI study with his colleague Christopher "Kit" Green, a neuroimaging specialist and former CIA agent instrumental in Stanford's remote viewing program; see sections 3.3 and 3.5. Green's background in the rigorous scientific study of psychic/spiritual reality is significant here as a complement to Nolan's strict materialism.

Analyzing the brains of people who have experienced UAP encounters, Nolan and Green

> found something right in the center that at first we thought was damage. It was an enriched patch of neurons that turned out to be living tissue with high neuronal connectivity. We think we found a form of higher functioning and processing. Kit Green has called these individuals "savants."[71]

Nolan and Green then discovered that this higher-than-typical integrative functioning not only runs in families, underscoring its genetic basis, but that it also tends to be shared by husband-wife couples. Given its rarity, this pairing suggests that intuitive savants are able to recognize and select one another.

In *Through the Curtain* (1983), Viola Petitt Neal, PhD, goes so far as to claim that

> this miniature brain for higher stages of development [contains] millions of antennae which in the future will [allow] for all the extrasensory perception, such as the ability to see events at a distance and the ability of telepathic contact. The sending and receiving station for telepathic contact is located in the caudate nucleus.[72]

Of course, such statements are currently far from provable, but interestingly, Garry Nolan has recommended this book.[73]

The psychically gifted "recruits" that Michael Herrera is talking about, who've been genetically singled out by means of blood tests, are given a very good life as working psionics. "Those in charge hook up to the psionics," Herrera explains. "The psionics then hook up to UAP pilots and translate back to our side. And they allow us to operate the vehicles."

To maximize performance, the psionics are medicated, "flooded with serotonin and other drugs, psychedelics, to boost their consciousness even higher." This manipulation takes a heavy toll; "these people do pass away over time. It's almost like they're in hospice, high and happy, but unaware they're actually dying."

A silver lining can be found, perhaps, in the promise for human evolution held out by even such an otherwise cruelly inhuman enterprise. Herrera asked an insider, "'What was the first thought that went through your mind when you learned about the P3 program?' He answered that it confirmed that there is an afterlife, which reassured him. There's a lot of spirituality involved."[74]

Chapter 6
UAPs and the Afterlife
A Shared Vibrational Neighborhood

I abandoned the extraterrestrial hypothesis in 1967, when my own field investigations disclosed an astonishing overlap between psychic phenomena and UFOs. To put it bluntly, the extraterrestrial theory is not strange enough to explain the facts. I believe there is a system around us that transcends time as it transcends space.
—Jacques Vallée, *Dimensions*

[The afterlife is] so rarefied that it is invisible to the mortal eye and eludes the finest instruments of the scientists. It is of the material universe.
—Frederic Myers, 1932, 31 years after bodily death, communicating through medium Geraldine Cummins

At this moment, you are surrounded by all kinds of energy [including] forms of energy on such high frequencies they cannot be detected with even the most sophisticated scientific instruments.
—John Keel, *The Cosmic Question*

When asked who they were, [the visitors] said that they were men composed, as it were, of air.
—Jacques Vallée, *Dimensions*

overview

- Circling back through some of our earlier themes, now equipped with more perspective.
- We look at why UAPs are less likely to come from elsewhere in the galaxy than from a higher frequency of reality, akin to spirits' frequency.

- Abductees' testimonials resonate strongly with both near-death experiences and the MTR theory, which is fascinating in itself, but it's no reason to believe the UAP occupants inhabit *our* afterlife.

6.1 Extraterrestrials, cryptoterrestrials, ultraterrestrials, oh my

I share Jacques Vallée's skepticism when it comes to our visitors' alleged origin in some distant star system. First of all, just look at them: The Grays are upright bipeds with two arms, two legs, hands, feet, a torso, neck, head, two eyes, two ears, a little nose and mouth in just the right spots, and we're supposed to believe they evolved independently on a foreign planet? And the other humanoids—the tall Grays, the Nordics, etc.—closely resemble us too. Even the more insectile or reptilian types appear to be variations on the same theme, still human-based but mixed with known Earth species. The kinship is undeniable; fundamentally, *they must have an intimate phylogenetic relationship to the genus Homo.*

We need to doubt the knee-jerk eagerness to take travel claims at face value. In *Dimensions*, Vallée writes,

> Many have declared that their home base has been identified: They come from a planet circling a star, Zeta Reticuli, in the southern constellation Reticulus. This is by no means the first time that the supposed origin of "flying saucers" has been revealed, either by the ufonauts themselves or by deduction from the words of the witnesses. In each case the witness seems genuinely sincere and believes in the "revelations." But in each case they contradict what other contactees are saying. The history of such identification goes back to the days of the 1897 airship, whose occupants invited witnesses to come with them to "a place where it doesn't rain." Asked where they were from, the strange pilots replied: "We're from anywhere, but we shall be in Greece tomorrow!" Another occupant mentioned Cuba. On July 23, 1947, near Pitanga, Brazil, a group of surveyors saw a disk-shaped craft land near them. One of them, Jose G. Higgins, saw three beings in translucent suits emerge from the saucer. They were

two meters tall with oversized bald heads. They drew the solar system for the benefit of the witness and pointed to Uranus as if to indicate they came from there. In 1952, a man named Truman Bethurum met space beings who claimed they originated from Clarion, a planet hidden from us by the sun.[75]

A competing theory, the one I subscribe to, is that our visitors are a species, genus, family, or entire kingdom of life form or forms that has or have shared our planet with us for untold eons. Commentators differ on the means by which they remain hidden. In *The Cryptoterrestrials: A Meditation on Indigenous Humanoids and the Aliens Among Us* (2010), Mac Tonnies writes, "Our relationship with these 'others' is far more widespread and intimate than even paranoid dramatizations of the UFO spectacle would have us believe."[76] Tonnies suggests that these fellow earthlings manage somehow to remain undetectable the vast majority of the time, emerging only when it suits them. He offers fascinating speculations on their behavior, agenda, and destabilizing trickery, but exactly how they stay unseen he doesn't say.

Another influential theorist, John Keel, best remembered for *The Mothman Prophesies*, articulated the same basic idea half a century ago, but he does provide a theoretical framework for their elusiveness. In *Operation Trojan Horse* (1970), Keel dubs the visitors *ultraterrestrials* and proposes that they and their ships are able to adjust their frequency along a vibrational *superspectrum*—which accounts for all of existence—coming and going at will to and from our limited slice of reality.

> The great majority of all sightings throughout history have been of "soft" luminous objects—objects that were transparent, translucent, changed size and shape, or appeared and disappeared suddenly.

To emphasize their dynamic nature, he calls these things "energies," though of course energy is just the flip side of matter.

> These energies coexist with us and even share the same space without our becoming acutely aware of them. UFO entities are directly related to the entities and manifestations involved in religious miracles and spiritual séances.[77]

You may notice the similarity to my matter-type ratio theory, MTR. "The phenomenon is mostly invisible to us," Keel writes, "because it consists of energy rather than solid Earthly matter. It makes itself visible to us from time to time by manipulating frequency."[78]

One difference, though, is that Keel's superspectrum is electromagnetic, an assumption that conflicts with more recent data. The visitors, he thinks, are "comprised of electromagnetic energy which can be manipulated to temporarily simulate terrestrial matter. Frequency changes are brought about to lower them into the visible spectrum."

The second difference is that, for Keel, this superspectrum leads straight up to ultimate being, which controls all that transpires beneath. This would make the visitors a direct manifestation of God, or Source, "the intelligent energy operating at the very highest possible point of the frequency spectrum, [which] might permeate the universe and maintain equal control over each component part."[79]

I see our UAP visitors as operating—like us and like our discarnate spirits—within the fundamental consciousness field (which produces IM). But for me, this field is one among many, not sitting at the top of a divine hierarchy; as we've seen, it can influence its fellow (OM-producing) fields, but it's neither their genesis nor in perfect Godlike "control over" them. The authority is contingent, not absolute. The field interactions can misfire; hence, the significant error rate in even the best psychics, mediums, and macro-PK practitioners—both incarnate and discarnate, earth-bound and sky-faring.

6.2 They're only human

Another sign of kinship between discarnate spirits and our visitors is a shared fallibility.

In *D. D. Home: His Life and Mission* (1888), another book I highly recommend, the medium's widow, Julie de Gloumeline, chronicles hundreds of remarkable physical phenomena that her husband was able to engender. Of one occasion, she writes,

> I expressed a wish to witness the actual production of a
> written message. A pencil and some sheets of paper
> had been lying on the centre of the table; presently the
> pencil rose up on its point, and, after advancing by

hesitating jerks to the paper, fell down. It then rose, and again fell. A third time it tried, but with no better result. After three unsuccessful attempts, a small wooden lath which was lying near upon the table slid towards the pencil and rose a few inches from the table; the pencil rose again, and propping itself against the lath, the two together made an effort to mark the paper. It fell, and then a joint effort was again made. After a third trial the lath gave it up and moved back to its place, the pencil lay as it fell across the paper, and an alphabetic message [with an early version of the Ouija board] told us—"We have tried to do as you asked, but our power is exhausted."[80]

Home's friend Windham Thomas Wyndham-Quin Adare also wrote a book about him, *Experiences in Spiritualism with D. D. Home* (1869). He describes another failed foray into macro-PK.

While moving, the table suddenly fell to the floor and rolled over. My clothes tumbled off, the money in the pockets rolling about the room. I said, "I wonder how it happened; it is so unusual for them to let anything fall." They answered [alphabetically], "It happened by mistake."[81]

Our visitors' own error rate is seen in occasional UAP crashes; John Mack observes that abductions don't always go off without a hitch.

Usually, abductees are returned to the bed or car from which they were taken, but sometimes "mistakes" are made. They may be returned...even miles away from their home. This is rare. Smaller mistakes are more common, such as landing the experiencer facing in the wrong direction on the bed, with his or her pajamas on backwards or inside out, or with certain garments or jewelry missing. Hopkins tells of a case where two abductees were returned to the wrong cars. As they drove along the highway the drivers recognized each other's cars. They were "re-abducted" and returned to the appropriate vehicles.[82]

6.3 Death, density, and close encounters of the fourth kind

The UFO abduction experience...bears resemblance to other dramatic, transformative experiences undergone by shamans, mystics, and ordinary citizens who have had encounters with the paranormal.
—John E. Mack, *Abduction*

If I could choose two words to sum up the UAP mystery, they would be "boundary dissolution."
—Jay Anderson of Project Unity

When we make the transition out of our earthly body, our spirit separates and rises. My explanation won't surprise you: *Up* is the direction of rapidly increasing IM/OM ratio; our spirit is lighter than air, seeking its level, its natural habitat. The process is no more esoteric, from a certain perspective, than a high school physics experiment. For discussion and examples, see Appendix D: Qi and Spirit. Here's an excerpt.

> Louisa May Alcott wrote of attending a deathbed vigil and watching "a light mist rise from the body, float up, and vanish in the air." Her mother saw it too. In *The Art of Dying*, Peter and Elizabeth Fenwick chronicle many such experiences. In the case of a woman attending the death of her sister: "I saw a fast-moving will-o'-the-wisp appear to leave her body by the side of her mouth. The shock and the beauty of it made me gasp. It appeared like a fluid or gaseous diamond, pristine, sparkly, and pure. It moved rapidly upwards and was gone."[83]

Above, in section 1.4, I touched on Mack's extensive work with UAP abductees. He distilled the main themes in two excellent books, *Abduction* (1994) and *Passport to the Cosmos* (1999). He focuses on cases in which abductees find themselves able to "let go" of their terror to some extent, enough to access the underlying emotional and spiritual texture of the experience.

In the context of this book, what strikes me most is how UAP witness descriptions resonate with the phenomenology of a spirit's passage at death and, accordingly, with MTR. After finding themselves in the presence of the visitors, usually the little Grays, abductees typically become paralyzed and then bullied into buoyancy, floated through the air and right *through* the bedroom wall, window glass, or car roof. This is predominantly a concrete, whole-body affair rather than a directed out-of-body transfer; they don't tend to see themselves still lying in bed.

This permeability of matter means that the matter-type ratio of the body itself, like that of a levitated table, is now forcibly tipped in favor of IM. *In Passport to the Cosmos*, Mack shares accounts that seem to bear this out. This is what it feels like to be suddenly flooded with IM—to be, in effect, an apport.

> Peter: "All the cells in my body are vibrating."
>
> Andrea: "I feel lightness. You lose your body. I'm melting. There's a lot of vibration…. I'm like expanding." [She] "floated feet first right through the glass of the window," which was "just amazing to me…. My body is expanding completely into the glass. The cells explode and expand, and that's how I go through the window. [It's as if] your body is finally awake. I believe we walk around in a sleeping condition…like our bodies, our cells are asleep."
>
> Sometimes the abductees will experience their own bodies as if they were filled with light or simply *were* light. The vibration may be quite intense, as if to fill all the experiencers' cells, which feel as if they are separating from each other or coming apart at the "molecular" level.
>
> Nona: "My energy in my entire body has been changed. It's like feeling cell against cell against cell…. I was just being loosened up."[84]

For their part, too, the visitors are free from gravity and able to pass through solid objects, floating alongside and conducting their captive. Low density seems to be their natural state.

> Jean: The beings were "very refined energy presences. They were literally beings of light."

Andrea: "They're very skinny, and they look like they're made of light. But underneath there's some physicalness to them like bones. They're not bones, though."[85]

6.4 *"We're not from here"*

Another consistent motif among abductees is the dawning conviction that Earth is not our true home, that our home is another level of reality, outside of space and time, and that our visitors, though freakish and bossy, hail from this other level. Mack writes that when recalling their brief sojourn,

> People are often drawn to what they call "Source" or "Home." And they will weep in my office when they are brought to the frustration that they can't be there all the time—they can't be home.[86]

We're familiar with an identical complaint among near-death experiencers. They are often infuriated when brought back to life, having just spent time in a domain "more real than real," a light-filled place where they profoundly belong.

In *Passport to the Cosmos*,

> Isabel regards her abduction experience as "a school to help you remember what you already know," which is that "we are all part of God but living in this backward structure. I don't know why these beings are helping us, but I'm glad they are. I had to go through all the terror. I had to go through letting go of everything, having everything shattered in my life. All of that was just a preparation for where spiritually I'm ready to start remembering everything. The remembrance program, the awakening program…I think they have actual steps."[87]

If these "steps" climb at least *toward* home, how far do they really go? Perhaps just far enough for us to catch a tantalizing whiff and to flirt with the winning vibration; after all, we, the helpless human cargo, always get summarily dumped back at the bottom of the staircase.

The kinship recognized, in sections 5.6 and 5.7, between UAP and psychic/spiritual phenomena is genuine, but to what extent do the two domains coincide? How far do they mount the density scale together? At what altitude do they part company?

6.5 Forms of contact

> *Tibetans distinguish between different gradations of subtlety and grossness (density) of beings. "The mind produced by grosser matter cannot communicate with these subtle things. In some, you witness the grosser level of mind subdued and the more subtle mind become active. Then there's an opportunity to communicate with or sometimes see another being who is more subtle."*
>
> —The Dalai Lama, 1992, quoted in John E. Mack, *Abduction*

Despite its drawbacks, I like John Keel's superspectrum for how it embraces and naturalizes the entire variegated landscape of what it's possible to experience. In the same spirit, Mack considers "the age-old gap between spirit and matter."

> The gap may be more apparent than real, growing out of our limited ways of knowing. It may be a "gap" only if we insist on trying to close it through physical measurement, or by seeing mechanisms familiar to us in the physical world, to understand the ways that the elements of the unseen realm(s) can become manifest.[88]

In other words, the less we strain after a solution using technology—our fancy, low-frequency toys—the better our chances at uncloaking the core problem. The same is true for UAPs; watch "Contact: The CE5 Experience" on the UNIDENTIFIED channel, in which people gather to "call in" our visitors by consciously resonating with them. CE5 stands for close encounters of the fifth kind. I also recommend "This Is Why CE5 Works" on the Project Unity channel, especially from the 42-minute mark. Jay Anderson describes his two 2019 encounters, each of which answered an intense, sincere desire for communion. Here is the second episode.

> About a month later, I saw these orbs again. They flew across the sky and stopped on a dime directly above me in the sky. And then they began to descend,

weaving in a dance-like motion. They were drifting down in quite a calming, non-threatening manner. And then they just stopped very abruptly, like someone had pressed pause. This was roughly three feet above the roof of my house. They were basketball-sized, a light pastel-orange color. Slightly transparent.

The next observation tracks with UAPs' documented lack of a heat signature; their form of energy is not dependent on the electromagnetic spectrum.

They weren't giving off light. There wasn't any sort of glow on my roof, and they themselves weren't glowing as you'd normally use that word. It was like a self-contained light. It's so hard to describe. It was almost as if they weren't really there.

They were there all right, but just in the liminal zone where words and conventional categories fail us. This is exactly how human spirits manifest as well, at the visibility threshold. The connection is direct and indirect at once, but no less *real* for all that.

"Spirit people have come in full physical form, stood beside me, and put their hands on my head," writes Edward C. Randall in *The French Revelation*. The book documents his lengthy study (1892-1914) of physical medium Emily French.

Their hands are firm, but the touch is strange because they are in a state of intense vibration; they do not tremble or shake, but they seem to pulsate with a rapidity that I have not words to describe.[89]

This placing of a buzzing hand on a researcher's head sounds to me like a quintessential laughing-off of the imaginary gulf between the living and the dead, a confluence of matter types with zero technology required. There's no separate dimension to access, no barrier to breach; the much-vaunted "veil" is a mere mirage, a shopworn dogma, a self-limiting state of mind.

In *The Afterlife Revolution*, Whitley Strieber's lovely meditation on his wife Annie, her death, and their ongoing communion, he exhorts the human race to overcome its blindness toward the actuality of the soul and its rarefied mode of existing. "A species is not whole," he writes, "unless a relationship between the living and the dead is an ordinary part of life."[90]

But there are steep challenges. Not every spirit can return to their former frequency at will. He quotes Annie as explaining, from her new perspective, that "getting to you is like swimming really deep. It feels like getting lost."

So, what is the role, if any, of the visitors? Strieber has often interacted with UAP occupants over the years, and sometimes they're accompanied by people he recognizes. "What about the dead that show up with the visitors?" he asks his wife. Annie answers,

> The visitors are practiced at moving back and forth between densities. When they tunnel down into your density, the human dead can follow them...to make those of you in the physical [condition] aware that we still exist. It's part of the fight against soul blindness.[91]

All that I've learned leads me to believe her. Here at depth where we reside, the cryptoterrestrials include both a cast of freakish, humanoid characters as well as beloved souls who have successfully taken the plunge to revisit us. Occasionally, the two cross paths, resonating, briefly sharing circumstances: "Going my way?" Since the UAPers are gifted at modulating their matter-type ratio, so much so that they appear and disappear constantly across the planet, amazing great crowds of earthlings and floating through our walls whenever they want to, then indeed it makes sense that they can offer us rides from up to down on the vibrational escalator, just as they carry some of us also from down to up for a fleeting taste of transcendence. We passengers find value in both directions.

The open question taunts us, though: What's the ticket price?

Epilogue
Why Earth?

During his near-death experience, Peter Panagore reports, "I was an orb of consciousness, thinking: Oh, now I remember: This *is me." He looked down on his lifeless body. "I can't believe I thought I was that* thing.*"*

Here at the end, let me put aside my reticence on the subject of the visitors' agenda and hazard a guess. First, some thoughts about our own purpose on this planet.

Why Earth 1: Us

When we make the transition, our scope of vision and understanding instantly breaks wide open. This is what I've learned from as many sources as possible; they all converge on a few salient points.

- New arrivals are bathed in an atmosphere of peace, welcome, light, and love—of being wholly known and accepted.
- We have an overwhelming sense of being "home" again, suddenly remembering that "*this* is where I belong"; this is real life, our genuine self, whereas our Earth life was just a dream, a pale reflection, a theater piece, a game, a school, a training ground or, as D. D. Home puts it, "a flash visit."
- We see and hear indescribable forms of utmost beauty—colors, landscapes, and music unlike those of Earth.
- We experience a vast expansion of our being, and yet we are surprised and relieved to find that we retain our selfhood, our essence, in all its unique aspects.
- And yet again, we immediately understand that we are just a tiny fraction of an infinite order and indissolubly connected to every other soul in existence; one near-death experiencer named Eddie saw numerous faces made of light: "I didn't recognize anybody from my life, but I *knew* everyone."
- Loved ones and other guides are here to help us every step of the way. We communicate directly, telepathically/emotionally; our minds and hearts are transparent to one another.

- Linear time as we knew it does not exist; instead, there's an ever-unfolding *right now*; distance, too, has disappeared; we can be anywhere instantly just by thinking of it, no travel time required. (This reality perfectly coincides with the block universe theory and quantum field theory; see Appendix A and Chapter 2.)
- Most religious dogma turns out to have been incorrect, a fear-driven, ego-driven distortion dominated by ingroup/outgroup thinking. God or Source plays no favorites. Love is "the great leveling wind." Each of us must come to terms with our own moral condition; no one else can "absolve" us of "sin"; for our personal moral burden, there is only remorse, contrition, and the opportunity for improvement, not divine judgment or punishment; Earth is a classroom, not a courtroom.
- The prime directive now is to learn and grow, and thereby to advance to higher states of existence, each of us evolving at our own pace. As we progress, our souls become less and less dense, made of purer and purer light, understanding, and love.

But if the afterlife is such a grand adventure, vastly superior to Earth life, why must we first endure this dense, bleak, and exhausting plane? Though dotted with beauty and moments of transcendence, most lives down here—unless highly privileged—are dominated by worry, fear, loss, and pain.

That's one way to look at it. Another is to recognize that even while trudging through this vale of tears, we're always already gaining ground on our soul's journey, whether we know it or not. And the laborious obstacle course itself is indispensable; a world without struggle is like a gym without weights.

Or a schoolhouse without work. We earthlings are here to learn and grow, even and *especially* in the worst of times. Pressure can break us, but pressure can also promote healing, as with a reset bone.

Life, a thick forest filled with beasts and risk, so little light getting through, could hardly be more different from the conditions that apparently await us—timeless and trouble-free. But our gift down here is time exactly, our chance to play the lead in an unfolding drama, and nothing's more interesting than trouble. God made us, wrote Elie Wiesel, "because He loves stories." What will happen next, and next? As the plot thickens, we're enlarged by the twists themselves, whatever their disposition; "The deeper that sorrow carves into your being," Kahlil Gibran reminds us, "the more joy you can contain."

If there were no such thing as Earth, how would we practice love, losing it and finding it, earning and wasting it again and again? Its value rises only through challenge.

Heaven's big on harmony, not so much on the bass drum of drama.

If there were no such thing as Earth, we'd never know this crowded, chaotic theater or the lush gravity of homesickness. The squeezing of the heart forms the meaning of its release.

Without Earth, no suspense, no thrum of possibility around every corner or the irreplaceable mainspring of youth, wild to discover, wild to flourish.

Why Earth 2: Them

> *It seems to me quite possible that the protection of the Earth's life is at the heart of the abduction phenomenon.*
> —John E. Mack, *Passport to the Cosmos*

> *My estimate is that we're looking at many thousands of* bone fide *sightings every year in the US and Canada. We are 5% of the world's population. Are we to think that all of the UAP action is happening here? There's no reason to think that. So, we're looking at a very, very heavy blanketing of our globe with these beings, with these craft. What are they doing? They may not be seeking to put us into a cookbook or to take over the world or instigate open warfare, but they are doing* something *that seems to be very, very important to them. They are everywhere. They are* everywhere.
> —Richard Dolan, UAP historian

> *[The abductee] said that whatever we humans are, we have a* soul *that is mysterious to them, and they are trying to find out: Where does the soul go at the moment of death?*
> —Linda Moulton Howe

> *The phenomenon is some form of human farming.*
> —Dr. Karla Turner, PhD, 1994 interview with Art Bell

My guess is they're not after our extermination, world domination, or Earth's natural resources. Instead, they seek what makes us... *us*. They ride here "from outside the stream of time," as Whitley Strieber puts it.

> This is why we're here. We're taking this journey, and it's very important not to see too far ahead because that would be like being dead and alive at the same time.
>
> They are much less dense than we are, and that's why when you're with them, there's no separation between the living and the dead. They know the future, so they are no longer *alive* in our sense: They can't have new experiences. And that could be one of the reasons they're here. That must be a nightmare, to be trapped in a reality where you can never experience anything new. No surprises. For us in our world, everything is always fresh.[92]

They pursue and connect with us in order to experience life vicariously—our particular species of hearty, knife-edge, eye-opening life. John Mack wrote, "I hear in a number of cases...that the alien beings envy our dense, physical embodiment."[93]

They float around us in their shapeshifting ships, in their stilted avatar bodies, citizens neither of pure spirit nor of panting animal spontaneity. Is this why they have been trying forever to merge with us? Strieber reports that most are automatons, "as accurate and as fast as machines." Other witnesses have compared them to "coldly efficient insects."

You'll recall those who felt their abductors were taking them "home [to] a place more real than real" and how this echoes NDE descriptions of the afterlife environment. It seems the meddling levitators do at least traffic in that same general vibrational neighborhood as our posthumous destination, so that when they take us away, we naturally receive the brief thrill of transcending Earth; any reprieve from dense matter and linear time is going to register as freedom from bondage, as ultimate arrival—but is it? Abductees don't have actual death yet to compare it with.

Strieber declares that "every single soul will ascend in the end...toward ecstasy." I doubt this applies to them, though; I'm pretty sure they're caught in the middle between authentic Earth life and eternal afterlife. For some reason, they are consigned to a narrow band on either side of the visibility threshold, on a perpetual mission, patrolling for what they lack, panning not for gold but for souls. If they enjoyed full latitude, all opportunity and grace—as rising human spirits do, lighter and lighter—would they constantly boomerang back to these heavy lowlands, hounding us day after day, millennium after millennium, from Ezekiel to the USS Nimitz?

The aliens are alienated.

They can't get up to Source because they can't first get fully grounded down here. As we marvel at their vehicles, we've been the secret vehicle all along. Ironically, while they seem to own the skies, they're trying to hitch a ride with *us* to even further heights.

However, "They have a problem," Strieber continues.

> We're in danger on two fronts: nuclear war and climate change. They might be asking themselves, "How do we help them out of this pickle without blowing our cover?" If they emerge directly, our whole race will turn toward them, latch onto them, and cease living our own adventure.[94]

In retrospect, have they ever lifted us to the afterlife itself, or even to the glorious, infinite vistas described by near-death experiencers? No, they deliver us instead to some austere way station; "I was suddenly in a place made of iron," reports Credo Mutwa. "It was sort of round, like a tank."[95] There, they paralyze and probe us, groping for that essential spark.

All of the dire ecological messages—telepathic scenes of environmental apocalypse and exhortations to restore and preserve our environment—may be as selfish as they are altruistic, or more so. In the face of our rank failure of planetary stewardship, they must safeguard this garden of souls in order to maintain access to their nourishment, their taproot, their chance at ecstasy.

References

1. Arthur Conan Doyle, *The Vital Message*, Broadman Press, New York: 1946.
2. Plutarch, *Lucullus*, Chapter 8
3. Jacques Vallée, *Dimensions: A Casebook of Alien Contact*, Contemporary Books, Chicago: 1988.
4. Ibid.
5. Louis Elizando, tothestars.media
6. CBSnews.com
7. Linda Moulton Howe, Earthfiles channel
8. "Researchers Set New Quantum Entanglement Distance Record," Ryan Whitwam, Extreme Tech, 2022.
9. "Quantum Fields: The Most Beautiful Theory in Physics!" on the Arvin Ash channel
10. David Tong, University of Cambridge, "What is Quantum Field Theory?"
11. "Particles, Fields and The Future of Physics—A Lecture by Sean Carroll" Fermilab channel
12. Freeman Dyson, *From Eros to Gaia*, Penguin Books, New York: 1995.
13. Carroll, op. cit.
14. Heinrich Päs, *The One: How an Ancient Idea Holds the Future of Physics*, Basic Books, New York: 2023.
15. "Does time exist? Carlo Rovelli and the quantum response," lecturesbureau.gr
16. "The Long Self with Eric Wargo" on the New Thinking Allowed channel
17. Dean Radin, *Entangled Minds*
18. Russell Targe and Harold Puthoff, "Information transmission under conditions of sensory shielding," *Nature* volume 251, 1974.
19. "How The CIA Trained Psychic Spies for 20 Years" on the Area52 channel
20. Annie Jacobsen, *Phenomena: The Secret History of the U.S. Government's Investigations into Extrasensory Perception and Psychokinesis*, Little, Brown and Company, New York: 2017.
21. E. Winchester Stevens, *The Watseka Wonder*, Religio-Philosophical Publishing House, Chicago: 1887.
22. Eric Wargo, The Nighshirt blog

23. Jacques Vallée and Eric Davis, "Incommensurability, Orthodoxy, and the Physics of High Strangeness: A 6-layer Model for Anomalous Phenomena," *Semantic Scholar*, 2003.
24. Psi Encyclopedia
25. "The Scientific Truth of Psychic Phenomena w/ Dean Radin" on the Unraveling the Universe channel
26. "Psychokinesis (PK) with Loyd Auerbach" on the New Thinking Allowed channel
27. Leslie Kean, *Surviving Death: A Journalist Investigates Evidence for an Afterlife*, Crown Archetype, New York: 2017.
28. Juan Gimeno and Dario Burgo, "Laboratory Research on a Presumably PK-Gifted Subject," *Journal of Scientific Exploration* Vol. 31, No. 2, 2017.
29. "Leslie Kean Returns—New UFO Revelations, Surviving Death Evidence, and More!" on the Chris Lehto channel
30. Irving Finkel, *The First Ghosts: Most Ancient of Legacies*, Hodder & Stoughton, London: 2019.
31. Avi Loeb, "How much do we know about what the universe is made of?", The Hill, 2022.
32. Edward Belbruno and James Green, "When leaving the solar system: Dark matter makes a difference," *Monthly Notices of the Royal Astronomical Society*, Volume 510, Issue 4, 2022
33. Jill Scudder, "How Dense Is Dark Matter?" Jillian Scudder, *Forbes Science*, 2017
34. Phases of Matter, NASA, www.grc.nasa.gov
35. William Crookes, *Researchers in the Phenomena of Spiritualism*, J. Burns, London: 1874.
36. Crawford, William, *The Reality of Psychic Phenomena*, E. P. Dutton & Co., New York: 1916.
37. Barrie G. Colvin, "The Acoustic Properties of Unexplained Rapping Sounds," *Journal of the Society for Psychical Research*, Vol 73.2, Number 899, 2010.
38. Julie de Gloumeline, *D. D. Home: His Life, His Mission*, K. Paul, Trench, Trubner & co., ltd, London: 1888.
39. Gimeno and Burgo, op. cit.
40. Phylameana lila Désy, *The Everything Guide to Reiki*, 2012.
41. Meade Layne, editor, *The Coming of the Guardians*, Inner Circle Press, San Diego, CA: 1956.
42. Grant Solomon and Jane Solomon, *The Scole Experiment:*

Scientific Evidence for Life After Death, Campion Books, Essex, UK: 1999.
43. N. Riley Heagerty, *The French Revelation: Voice to Voice Conversations with Spirits Through the Mediumship of Emily S. French*, White Crow Books, Guildford, UK: 2015.
44. Illobrand von Ludwiger and Michael Nahm, "Apport phenomena of medium Herbert Baumann: Report on personal experiences," *Journal of Scientific Exploration*, 2016.
45. Ibid.
46. Ibid.
47. Ibid.
48. Stewart Alexander, *An Extraordinary Journey: The Memoirs of a Physical Medium*, White Crow Books, Surrey, UK: 2020.
49. Ibid.
50. Ibid.
51. Eileen Garrett, *My Life as a Search for the Meaning of Mediumship*, Oquaga Press, New York: 1939.
52. Klaus Heinemann and Micheál Ledwith, *The Orb Project*, Atria Books, New York: 2007.
53. Kean, op. cit.
54. James T Lacatski, Colm A Kelleher, George Knapp, *Skinwalkers at the Pentagon: An Insiders' Account of the Secret Government UFO Program*, RTMA, Llc: 2021.
55. "A Tear in the Sky" on the Unidentified channel
56. NASA.com
57. Lacatski, Kelleher, Knapp, op. cit.
58. Ibid.
59. Ibid.
60. Ibid.
61. "George Knapp Λ Colm Kelleher: Skinwalkers, Hitchhiker Effect"on the Theories of Everything with Curt Jaimungal channel
62. Vallée, op. cit.
63. Twitter post by planethunter56, September 4, 2023.
64. "Jack Sarfatti - Congressional UFO Hearing" on the Tim Ventura channel
65. Jon Plus, *UAP Propulsion: A Metamaterial Approach to Spacetime Control*, 2023.
66. "Do we Share Earth with Someone Else—Garry Nolan" on the Event Horizon channel
67. "Expanding Our Understanding On UAP Technology –

with Scientist Garry Nolan" on the Merged Podcast channel
68. Ibid.
69. Ibid.
70. "Inside the Secret Government UFO Retrieval Program Part 1" on the Chris Lehto channel
71. "What UFO encounters teach us about the brain | Garry Nolan and Lex Fridman" on the Lex Clips channel
72. *Through the Curtain*, Viola Petitt Neal, Ph.D., and Shafica Karagulla, M.D., Devorss & Company, Marina Del Rey, CA: 1983.
73. "Extrasensory Perception and the Caudate Nucleus" on The Mind Sublime blog
74. Chris Lehto interview, op. cit.
75. Vallée, op. cit.
76. Mac Tonnies, *The Cryptoterrestrials: A Meditation on Indigenous Humanoids and the Aliens Among Us*, Anomalist Books, Lexington, KY: 2011.
77. John Keel, *Operation Trojan Horse*, Manor Books, New York: 1970.
78. Ibid.
79. Ibid.
80. Gloumeline, op. cit.
81. Windham Thomas Wyndham-Quin Adare, *Experiences in Spiritualism with D. D. Home*, London: 1886.
82. John E. Mack, *Abduction: Human Encounters with Aliens*, Ballantine Books, New York: 1995.
83. Wargo, The Nightshirt blog
84. John E. Mack, *Passport to the Cosmos: Ηuman Transformation and Alien Encounters*, Crown Publishers, New York: 1999.
85. Ibid.
86. Ibid.
87. Ibid.
88. Ibid.
89. Heagerty, op. cit.
90. Whitley Strieber, *The Afterlife Revolution*, Walker & Collier: 2017.
91. Ibid.
92. "UFOs, Non-Human Intelligence, Consciousness, the Afterlife & Anomalous Experiences: Whitley Strieber" on the Unraveling the Universe channel
93. Mack, 1999, op. cit.
94. Strieber, Unraveling the Universe channel interview.
95. Mack, 1999, op. cit.

Appendix A
Einstein's Block Universe and the Illusion of Linear Time

The following discussion is quite in the weeds. The purpose is to account theoretically for the empirical fact that people can sometimes know the future. They are not *predicting* the future; they are directly accessing it at a highly detailed level, just as remote viewers access information nonlocally. Remote viewers would not be able to access this information if it didn't exist; by the same token, precognition/clairvoyance could not access information about the future if the future did not already exist. For concrete examples, see Chapter 3 of *There Is No Veil* and the article in Psi Encyclopedia, "Precognition."

* * *

In classical Newtonian physics, the universe as a whole exists in a single time frame—the present moment—making the past and the future both nonexistent; the absolute *now* alone is real. This conception was overturned by Einstein in 1905 when his theory of special relativity demonstrated that there is in fact no privileged now, that the idea of a present moment can have meaning only with respect to a single observational frame of reference. What for me is an event occurring now would to another observer, located elsewhere, occur in the past, and to still a third observer, in the future. But how can this be?

As physicist Kip Thorne puts it, "Einstein's great insight was to recognize that time and space are *personal*." That is, their measured qualities are founded on observational perspective.

Say you have a long row of firecrackers before you, marked A through Z, and you set them all off at exactly the same moment. You would witness one uniform area of space hosting one event—multiple simultaneous explosions. But actually, it's a *mixture* of space and time, because if another observer, say I, were flying past you ten miles away at great speed, I would see the lights of all those firecrackers going off at slightly different times in a series, A to Z. This is because the speed of light is finite.

Then, add a third observer, Caroline, also ten miles from you and traveling at great speed in the direction opposite to mine. From her perspective, the firecrackers will also ignite sequentially, but now from Z to A.

Expand the distances among we three observers enough, and increase our relative motion, and the time discrepancies will grow more and more significant until what for you will remain twenty-six simultaneous flashes will come to appear, for me and for Caroline, to happen farther and farther apart. If we zoom past and away from them at an angle and continue to accelerate, they will flash years apart…then centuries…etc.

And here is the startling corollary: For you, firecracker flashes A-Z all occur in the present; for me, when flash A occurs in my present, flashes B-Z are still in my future; for Caroline, by the time she experiences flash A, flashes Z-B are already in her past. In other words—and by extension for the whole universe—past, present, and future are entirely relative qualities, none any less real or objective than the others.

This breakthrough recognition of temporal elasticity turns out to apply even more broadly to reality as such; yet another false boundary gets removed. Not only are time and space personal, answering to reference frames alone, but they also turn out to be but two aspects of a single all-pervasive whole. Instead of Newton's absolute time and (separately) three-dimensional space, what emerges from Einstein's insight is a staggeringly novel conception—four-dimensional spacetime.

It's a worldview nearly impossible to wrap one's head around because everyday experience offers no helpful illustrations; our brains did not evolve, on the African savannah, to compute anything remotely of the kind. At first blush, though, it's easy to say, "Okay, right, so it's not three dimensions anymore but four. Four instead of three, no big deal." But to actually, concretely grasp the fact that *time itself*—an invisible abstraction—is somehow on equal footing with the direct evidence of our senses—say, the length, breadth, and depth of that red brick in your hands—is a bridge too far for most. At the macro level, however, as velocities approach the speed of light and distances stretch into light-years, the integration becomes obvious. As NASA astronomer Michelle Thaller explains, "Your time changes, in contrast to others', depending on how fast you're moving through space with respect to them. The faster you go, the slower time appears to be moving *for you from their perspective*," though you won't experience the deceleration as such, for the simple reason that *your* time (subjective experience) slows down, so you will always know it at the rate of one second per second.

By the same token, of course, through your eyes the "movie" of the rest of the universe will continue to speed up. Therefore, according to Neil deGrasse Tyson, "As you arrive at 99.9999999% the speed of light, you can watch the entire history of the universe unfold during what for you are only a few seconds."[1]

Incidentally, though such wild propositions may seem merely speculative or theoretical, they are as real and immediate as that same red brick in your hand. Even at more familiar speeds, the effect can be measured. Atomic clocks have documented the warping of time when placed aboard jets, as in the 1971 Hafele–Keating experiment. And as reported in the *Scientific American* article "How Time Flies: Ultraprecise Clock Rates Vary with Tiny Differences in Speed," newly developed optical clocks are so precise that they can register the passage of time differently at velocities of a just few meters per second. The faster one object moves through the three dimensions of physical space—*at any speed*—the more slowly it moves through the fourth dimension, time, relative to another object.

We can visualize the fabric of spacetime, then, as an organic whole, two aspects of the same thing, like yin and yang. Thaller continues,

> Einstein illustrated this by showing that you have to adjust space and time so they always balance out, *mutually conserve or constrain one another*. If I start accelerating, my time slows down with respect to yours, which is compensating for my motion through space; since I'm moving through space very fast, I can't move through time as fast as I would otherwise.
>
> Einstein believed that the beginning of the universe, the Big Bang, created all of space and all of time at

once, so that every point in the past and every point in the future is just as real as the point of time you feel yourself to be in right now. He believed that literally. Time is a landscape, and if you had the right perspective on the universe, you would see all of it laid out in front of you.

One of his best friends died, and he wrote a letter to this friend's wife saying that the man still existed. He wrote to the wife that her husband was just over the next hill. "He has departed from this strange world a little ahead of me. That means nothing. For us convinced physicists, the distinction between past, present, and future is only a stubbornly persistent illusion." You yourself have been dead for billions of years, and you haven't been born yet.[2]

According to Einstein and many other renowned cosmologists—e.g., Minkowski, Putnam, Rietdijk, and Smart—all of this points inexorably to a universe in which, essentially, "nothing *happens*; everything already *is*." This outlook is known as *eternalism* (as contrasted with presentism, in which time is linear and sequential, and only the current moment is real). The vantage point taken here is often termed the "God's-eye perspective," which is meant logically rather than theologically—a way of saying "from the greatest conceivable distance, both physically and intellectually."

The "landscape" analogy above is a version of what has also been called the "block universe," the postulation that, as seen through this maximalist lens, the entirety of spacetime forms a single four-dimensional block. Objects—including the human body—are extended through its time dimension just as they are extended spatially; all persisting objects are four-dimensional "worldlines" that stretch across spacetime; no object is merely three-dimensional, and each of our life stories amounts to what Eric Wargo calls "the long self."[3]

The trouble with this image, though, is that it conveys an impression of fixity, as in a block of concrete with everything locked in place. It's a challenge to reconcile this notion with the dynamism of the cosmos and the events unfolding here on Earth. But this problem is ours, not the theory's. It's only in the broadest sense that "nothing happens; go any narrower and plenty happens. The trick is to recognize that change and history—at every level, in all their rich, advancing animation—are baked into the very essence of the block as such. Why? Because it includes time, and time and change are indistinguishable.

Some believe that the block universe theory has come and gone, that it's been superseded by new developments in cosmology. On the contrary, though, it is still very much in play, as evidenced by the recent high-profile publication of *Beyond the Dynamical Universe: Unifying Block Universe Physics and Time as Experienced* (Oxford University Press, 2018).

Referernces

1. "Time: Do the past, present, and future exist all at once?", the Big Think YouTube channel.
2. Ibid.
3. Eric Wargo, *Time Loops*, Anomalist Books, Charlottesville, Virginia: 2018.

Appendix B
The Experimental Evidence for Parapsychological Phenomena: A Review

Etzel Cardeña, *American Psychologist*, Vol 73(5), Jul-Aug 2018.

Abstract

This article presents a comprehensive integration of current experimental evidence and theories about so-called parapsychological (psi) phenomena. Throughout history, people have reported events that seem to violate the commonsense view of space and time. Some psychologists have been at the forefront of investigating these phenomena with sophisticated research protocols and theory, while others have devoted much of their careers to criticizing the field. This article clarifies the domain of psi, summarizes recent theories from physics and psychology that present psi phenomena as at least plausible, and then provides an overview of recent/updated meta-analyses. The evidence provides cumulative support for the reality of psi, which cannot be readily explained away by the quality of the studies, fraud, selective reporting, experimental or analytical incompetence, or other frequent criticisms. The evidence for psi is comparable to that for established phenomena in psychology and other disciplines, although there is no consensual understanding of it.

People in all walks of life have reported events that seem to violate the current commonsense view of space and time, from dreams that seem to ostensibly predict a non-inferable, dramatic event, to the more mundane assertion by a former prime minister of Sweden that he can sense when his wife is about to call him (Thunberg, 2006). In various surveys, majorities of respondents have endorsed a belief in such phenomena, which may have a noticeable impact on their lives (Watt

& Tierney, 2014). In the last few years, parapsychology (psi) research has appeared in major psychology journals (e.g., Bem, 2011; Storm, Tressoldi, & Di Risio, 2010a, 2010b), and comprehensive reviews of the evidence for and against psi have been published (Cardeña, Palmer, & Marcusson-Clavertz, 2015; May & Marwaha, 2015), but no recent integration of current theories and evidence has been published.

Some psychologists have been at the forefront of producing supportive research and theory; others have devoted much of their careers to criticizing the field. Both stances can be explained by psychologists' expertise on relevant processes such as perception, memory, belief, and conscious and nonconscious processes. However, many psychologists probably lack solid knowledge of the area. An informed psi skeptic wrote, "Most psychologists could reasonably be described as uninformed skeptics—a minority could reasonably be described as prejudiced bigots—where the paranormal is concerned" (French, 2001, p. 7). It is thus important to have an overview and discussion of the research and theory on the topic. This article will (a) introduce the domain of psi research; (b) discuss relevant theoretical frameworks from physics, psychology, and evolutionary theory; (c) review recent/updated meta-analyses in the field; and (d) provide guidelines for future research.

The domain of psi research

From the founding in 1882 of the Society for Psychical Research, research on psi has used or even developed scientific practices, with the aim to "examine without prejudice or prepossession" the nature of these phenomena. *Parapsychology* can be defined as the study of purported psi phenomena using the scientific method, and the Parapsychological Association, the professional association of the field, has been an affiliate of the American Association for the Advancement of Sciences (the world's largest general scientific society) since 1969.

Psi typically includes two major areas: (1) what used to be called extrasensory perception, or ESP, and (2) psychokinesis, or PK. ESP includes purported *telepathy* (being affected by someone's thoughts or emotions, unmediated by the senses or logical inference, such as guessing more accurately than would be expected by chance who sends you an e-mail unexpectedly), *clairvoyance* (obtaining information about a distant state of affairs, unmediated by the senses or logical inference, such as in *remote viewing* (RV) in which someone accurately describes details of a place chosen at random by someone else), *precognition/presentiment* (being affected by an event taking a place in the future that could not have been foreseen, as in dreaming about planes crashing against tall buildings the night before 9/11), and *retrocognition* (having noninferable knowledge about a past event). *ESP* is a misleading term because it suggests perception as the mediating mechanism, although few if any psi researchers nowadays assume this to be the case. Furthermore, the distinction among these phenomena is a function of how they are tested or considered rather than of different mechanisms. Examples labeled as *clairvoyance* could also be considered as *telepathy*, and both of them could be subsumed under *precognition*, because someone at some point in the future will find out that information. The term *anomalous cognition* will be used in this article (Cardeña et al., 2015; May, Utts, & Spottiswoode, 1995).

PK refers to putative direct action of mental events (e.g., intention) on physical objects, unmediated by muscular or indirect mechanical activity. There is *macropsychokinesis* (or *anomalous force*), an effect on observable objects such as a table levitating without any apparent mechanical explanation, and *micropsychokinesis* (or *anomalous perturbation*), an effect on small, unobservable events, such as mentally affecting the output of a random number generator that otherwise produces random outputs. Some psi researchers study the possibility of consciousness surviving death, including studies of children who spontaneously report information about a past life to which neither they or those close to them apparently had access (Mills & Tucker, 2015), but which have also been interpreted as examples of anomalous cognition rather than of survival (Sudduth, 2009). Both descriptive and experimental approaches can be employed to evaluate psi phenomena.

At its inception, psychology and parapsychology were not clearly distinct disciplines, and foundational figures of the former also supported the latter (Cardeña, 2015a; Sommer, 2013. They include Bekhterev, Hans Berger (inventor of the electroencephalogram), Binet, Fechner, Sigmund Freud, Luria, Ramón y Cajal, and American

Psychological Association (APA) presidents William James and Gardner Murphy. More recently, faculty from top-ranked universities such as Harvard, Princeton, and Stanford, including a past APA president, endorsed continuing research on psi (Cardeña, 2014).

Parapsychology has also contributed to methods and subject areas later integrated into psychology, among them the first use of randomization along with systematic use of masking procedures (Hacking, 1988); the first comprehensive use of meta-analysis, in 1940 (Gupta & Agrawal, 2012); study preregistration since 1976 (Johnson, 1976); and pioneering contributions to the psychology of hallucinations, eyewitness reports, and dissociative and hypnotic phenomena (for a review, see Hövelmann, 2015).

Psi phenomena and physics theories

Because psi phenomena are sometimes assumed a priori to violate physics principles, three common objections will be discussed, namely that (1) they violate the "laws of nature"; (2) if accepted, they would invalidate scientific achievements; and (3) there are no theories to account for them. What is often meant by psi critics as violations of the laws of nature involves assumptions about an event not being able to affect another at a distance without some mediating form of known energy, future events being unable to affect previous ones, and mental events not having direct effects on other than the organism privy to them. However, quantum mechanics (QM) and Einstein's theory of relativity have depicted a reality that differs substantially from commonsensical assumptions. Nobel laureate and pioneer of molecular biology Max Delbrück (1986) expressed it so: "Modern science . . . has forced us to abandon absolute space and time, determinism, and the absolute object" (p. 279).

Nonlocality

In his interpretation of QM (and experts differ on how to interpret it, e.g., Schlosshauer, Kofler, & Zeilinger, 2013), the eminent physicist Bernard d'Espagnat (1979, 2006) discussed the implications of experiments showing that measuring/observing the property of a particle, such as its spin, *instantaneously* determines that of another particle entangled with it, no matter how distant. Entanglement means that the quantum states of such particles are not independent but part of a system, which can be produced in different ways. D'Espagnat concluded that such experiments falsify the local realist theory that effects cannot propagate faster than light and that objects far apart in space are relatively independent. For him, the world is not made of separate "material" objects embedded in space-time, but of a nonseparable, indivisible field, a "veiled reality," with which consciousness interacts. He concluded that the implications of QM and "transcendentalism-inclined thinkers" (d'Espagnat, 2006, p. 429) have points in common, as did renowned physicist David Bohm (1986) in his theory of the *implicate order* or guiding field, which he applied to psi phenomena.

Scientific American journalist George Musser (2015) also supported a nonlocal interpretation of QM and considered space "a doomed concept" (p. 125). He also described how effects violating assumptions of locality do not occur exclusively at the particle but also at the cosmic level (and at the mesolevel of living beings; see Lambert et al., 2013). Along these lines, Princeton physics philosopher Hans Halvorson concluded that a form of *superentanglement* links every aspect of everything in the universe (Musser, 2015, p. 139). In principle, thus, psi phenomena—such as a sudden death affecting a loved one at another location—are consistent with a nonlocal view of the universe. Furthermore, as compared with classical physics, which depicts a universe where everything is determined by previous causes, QM proposes that before there is a collapse of the quantum wave function by some type of measurement, objects are only probability functions (Musser, 2015). In parapsychology, observational theories propose that psi experiments exploit the indeterminacy of a system, which may become slightly biased by the intention of an observer (Millar, 2015), or as Stapp (2017) put it, by "relevant conditions that include the experienced emotions of biological agents" (p. 106).

Time

Einstein's theories of time and the ensuing experiments demonstrated that objectively measured time and space are not absolute and depend on such variables as the position and speed of the observers and the gravitational field. For instance, events that are still in the future of a slow-moving individual may have already occurred to a faster moving one; furthermore, in the special relativity block universe theory of time, past, present, and future coexist simultaneously although we experience only the present (Davies, 2002). Despite our typical perception of time as only an ever-receding series of moments, experiments on quantum retrocausality (or backward causation) suggest that future events may affect previous ones. For example, measuring the spin of a particle, which collapses its probabilistic wave function into a determinate value, seems to retroactively determine the spin of a delayed photon entangled with it. Physicist Daniel Sheehan (2011, 2015) concluded that experiments in physics and psi support retrocognitive effects, and physicist and parapsychologist Edwin May has developed a theory in which signals from a future space-time point, such as having eventual knowledge of the target of an experiment, may affect previous cortical processes of those trying to guess it (e.g., Marwaha & May, 2016). An alternative explanation is that consciousness may bias a future event (Stapp, 2017).

Consciousness

One of the interpretations of QM requires that the measurement that makes a wave function of probabilities collapse into a determinate outcome be made by a sentient observer (Stapp, 2017). Consistent with a causal role for sentience, Delbrück (1986) criticized "the Cartesian cut between mind and matter" (p. 279), and cognitive psychologist Max Velmans (2000) also discussed the reasons why a hard distinction between "objective" and "subjective" phenomena is misguided. Along these lines, a professor of cosmology wrote that "the materialist position in physics appears to rest on shaky metaphysical ground" (Frank, 2017, quoted from the subtitle) and questioned the materialist stance in the neurosciences to explain consciousness. Renowned philosopher of mind Thomas Nagel (2012) concluded that the explanatory gap between neurochemical processes and mental experiences is difficult to resolve from a materialist, evolutionary perspective and that reality is not reducible to material, mental, or functional realms, but subsumes them all. Princeton physicist Freeman Dyson (1988, p. 297) ascribed different levels of mind from the particle to the cosmic levels, and Velmans (2000) concluded that a continuous model of sentience is more parsimonious than one proposing that mentality just emerges from matter at some level of complexity. To add eminent neuroscientists to those who endorse nonmaterialist views of mind, Christof Koch, an earlier collaborator of arch-reductionist Francis Crick (Crick & Koch, 1990), concluded with Giulio Tononi that consciousness is a fundamental property of information in complex entities (Tononi & Koch, 2015, see also Dyson, 1988; Kelly, 2015).

But how might "mental" events interact with "physical" ones, assuming that they differ ontologically? University of London professor of mathematics and cosmology Bernard Carr (2015) has described recent hyperspatial or hyperdimensional approaches that posit additional dimensions beyond the temporal and three-spatial ones. He proposes that events that seem to be distant in our three-dimensional space may be adjacent in a hyperdimensional one, and that the dichotomy between mind and matter of common sense is resolved by a hyperdimensional "transcendental field" in which mental phenomena can have causal effects. Lawrence Livermore National Laboratory physicist Henry P. Stapp (2017, p. 65) has developed a "realistically construed orthodox quantum mechanics" model in which conscious intentions can produce a small bias on quantum processes, and indeed research has shown significant small effects of intention on photon wave patterns (Radin, Michel, & Delorme, 2016).

The above views do not "prove " that psi phenomena exist but makes them plausible, and some physicists have proposed specific theories for them. They are also a response to psychologists who state that psi phenomena are impossible. "Parapsychologists believe in 'impossible' things" (Alcock, 2010, p. 29); "psi conflicts with what we know to be true about the world" (Wagenmakers, Wetzels, Borsboom, & Van der Maas, 2011, p. 46).

Psychological and evolutionary theories of psi
Two psychological theories, psi-mediated instrumental response (PMIR; Stanford, 2015) and first-sight theory (Carpenter, 2012), seek to integrate psi with psychological and evolutionary theories. Although varying in details, both propose that psi information

continuously, although usually nonconsciously, impinges on mental processes and may serve adaptive and/or personal inclinations. PMIR has been the basis for studies in which rewarding psi tasks embedded within nonpsi experiments were found to affect performance in experiments (see section on implicit anomalous cognition below). A premise of PMIR is that an organism may respond to events outside of its sensory reach if it would respond to them if they were perceivable, such as avoiding an unperceivable dangerous situation, and there is a motivational component to what the organism will likely attend to depending on its particular dispositions and schemata (Stanford, 2015). Similarly, according to the first-sight model: (a) psi is not limited by the commonsensical view of time and space and is fundamental to all organisms, and (b) it mostly operates nonconsciously but may affect consciousness and action in accordance with the organism's dispositions (Carpenter, 2012).

There are also explanations of why alterations of consciousness have been found to relate to psi. According to the "noise reduction" theory, psi information is subtle and likely to remain nonconscious in the midst of the overwhelming information provided by the senses and bodily actions unless these inputs are reduced (Honorton, 1977). Thus, procedures that reduce these stimuli—such as meditation, hypnosis, and ganzfeld—should facilitate awareness of psi (see the sections on ganzfeld and dream research below). Besides restriction of sensory input, alterations in consciousness may make awareness of psi more likely by reducing critical thought and stimulating a sense of interconnectedness (Cardeña, 2010).

Psi has also been discussed from an evolutionary perspective. According to Broughton (2015), psi should be seen in the larger context of biological processes including brain functioning and evolution. He stated that psi is a correlation between future and previous events that could have been maintained even providing as little as a 1% fitness advantage. This small effect could subtly affect decisions through hunches and similar mechanisms, consistent with the small effects found in research. Research and observations in nature support the existence of psi in other species (Safina, 2015; Sheldrake, 2015).

As to statements such as the one by a cognitive scientist that accepting psi phenomena would "send all of science as we know it crashing to the ground" (Hofstadter, 2011, para. 9) the most sensible answer is that psi phenomena are compatible with some interpretations by eminent physicists and manifest small effects that in no way invalidate the accomplishments of current science (Stapp, 2017). The Office of Technology Assessment (1989) report concluded that it is important to find out how psi can obtain "a fairer hearing across a broader spectrum of the scientific community, so that emotionality does not impede objective assessment of experimental results" (p. 337).

Summary of meta-analyses on psi

This section summarizes recent or updated comprehensive meta-analyses of psi research found through a recent comprehensive anthology that reviewed meta-analyses in the field (Cardeña et al., 2015), contacts with parapsychology researchers, and an additional literature search. The latter used two databases, PsycInfo and Medline, without language or year restriction. The search produced about 20 nonoverlapping items, many of them not meta-analyses but comments about them. All comprehensive recent/updated meta-analyses found are discussed below along with more limited but relevant ones. Although meta-analyses have limitations that may affect their results (e.g., a potential publication bias), they contribute to knowledge of established and contentious areas (Chan & Arvey, 2012). The primary sources in the meta-analyses reviewed here include alternative and comprehensive analyses and evaluate variables that might have impacted the data, including the design quality and homogeneity of the studies, and potential publication biases.

Anomalous cognition

In anomalous cognition research, participants "guess" a randomly chosen target from a known (e.g., a set of cards) or unknown (e.g., a film clip from a large sample) set without information from the senses or logical inference. It includes two main models of research: free response and forced choice (for a review of safeguards commonly used to avoid confounds such as sensory leakage and judging bias see Palmer, 2015a).

Free response

In free-response studies, the target that the masked raters will evaluate is not part of a set known to them such as a deck of cards, but of a large or undetermined dataset, such as a photo or film clip from an unknown large or open set (e.g., the stimuli may come from a pool of dozens of clips including animated, documentary, or feature films, or a location chosen at random). Various types of free-response protocols have been studied.

Ganzfeld is a German term for "whole field." In psi research, it refers to a procedure in which the participant sits in a comfortable chair and listens to physical relaxation instructions and exposure to white or pink noise (unpatterned random frequencies, similar to the sound between radio stations), with two acetate ovals covering the eyes in front of which red light bulbs produce the effect of shapeless redness. The participant's task is to become aware of an unknown image or clip chosen randomly, which might be shown simultaneously in a distant computer with nobody watching it (clairvoyance), someone watching it (telepathy), or is chosen *after* the participant makes a selection (precognition). The psi ganzfeld technique is based on the "noise reduction" theory mentioned above.

Research on ganzfeld has been meta-analyzed repeatedly and is the most consistently supportive database for psi of the last few decades. The methodological development of ganzfeld research followed a joint communiqué by psi-critic Ray Hyman and psi-proponent Charles Honorton (Hyman & Honorton, 1986) on how to conduct the experiments. The most recent and comprehensive meta-analyses of the database by Storm et al. (2010b) and Williams (2011) supported a psi effect. An earlier and more limited meta-analysis by Milton and Wiseman (1999) did not find a significant effect, but had they used the (apparently indicated) exact binomial test, it would have (Storm et al., 2010b, p. 473).

Table 1 shows the meta-analyses for (a) the aggregation of a comprehensive previous database (Storm & Ertel, 2001) with the newer database and for (b) the newer database alone (Storm et al., 2010b) for all studies, along with analyses for (c) the aggregation of all homogeneous combined studies and for (d) the homogeneous newer database, for which an outlier with a very high supportive z score was excluded. For the latter, *selected* participants (based on previous experience with the protocol and/or traits associated with psi performance such as being a meditator) had a bigger effect size, $ES = 0.26$, than their counterparts, $ES = 0.05$, $t(27) = 3.44$, $p = .002$. Williams (2011) reported that in ganzfeld participants guess around 31% of the time the correct target out of four choices presented in random order, when mean chance expectation would be 25%.

Hyman (2010) criticized the Storm et al. meta-analysis, claiming that meta-analyses should be conducted prospectively and that psi cannot be shown on demand. He also described a ganzfeld study that did not replicate the effect, although he disregarded others that did. Storm et al. (2010a) responded that other accepted phenomena in science cannot be produced on demand, and that retrospective meta-analyses are routinely used in science.

Rouder, Morey, and Province (2013) conducted a Bayesian probability analysis of the newer Storm et al. dataset excluding studies that had used manual instead of computerized randomization. They concluded that the Bayesian factor decreased from 6 billion to 1 to circa 330 to 1, but that because of a lack of a plausible mechanism and the possibility of unpublished replication failures, the meta-analysis did not support psi. They added, however, that the degree of evidence was "greater than that provided in many routine studies in cognition" (p. 245). Storm, Tressoldi, and Utts (2013) conducted a Bayesian analysis *not* excluding studies that had used random tables, as Rouder et al. (2013) had done, and concluded that their results did support a psi effect. Baptista, Derakhshani, and Tressoldi (2015) conducted additional analyses on the ganzfeld data that ratified a psi effect and rectified general claims that (a) when ganzfeld study quality goes up, ES goes down (actually, the opposite seemed to be the case), (b) ES had decreased in more recent studies (it has not), (c) psi generally declines in the course of a long study (it does not), and (d) a file-drawer analysis of a reasonable number of unreported nonsignificant results would annul the significant results (it does not).

In *implicit anomalous cognition* studies, volunteers respond to a psychological task, with a hidden psi aspect to it. As an example, in one study, participants were part of a research dyad and one of them had to indicate esthetic preference for Kanji Japanese characters. Unbeknownst to them, they were being tested for a psi target selected randomly. When participants chose the psi character target, their research partners did a more pleasant task than those whose partners did not select the psi target (Watt & Nagtegaal, 2000). The outcome variable was whether participants chose the target more often than would be expected by chance. Although there has not been a meta-analysis of these studies, Palmer (2015b, p. 227) concluded in a review that studies with a hidden reward had more significant outcomes than would be expected by chance.

Related to this paradigm, studies designed by Cornell psychologist Daryl Bem (2011) tested the hypothesis that a future stimulus might have a retroactive influence on a previous response. Bem took mainstream priming studies, in which a preceding word or image affects an ensuing response, and "time-reversed" them so that the word or image is presented *after* the response of the volunteer. For instance, one of his tasks evaluated whether a valence-consistent or inconsistent word affects the response time of a *preceding* image. Bem (2011) reported on nine different protocols with more than 1,000 participants and found that all but one of them was independently significant and that the mean *ES* was significant (the analyses were one-tailed, but they would have remained significant with two-tailed tests). Thus, the results supported the interpretation that a stimulus occurring later may influence a previous response more often than would be expected by chance.

Bem's studies, published in a major psychology journal, caused a storm of commentaries (Cardeña, 2015b). A meta-analysis of two of Bem's experiments, along with attempted replications by the authors of the article and by other investigators, concluded that a Bayesian analysis showed no psi effect (Galak, LeBoeuf, Nelson, & Simmons, 2012). Table 1 shows a larger a meta-analysis of all replication attempts until then, 90 experiments from 33 laboratories at the time of publication (Bem, Tressoldi, Rabeyron, & Duggan, 2015). The overall effect was significant (as was a Bayesian analysis), and the *ES* for the complete database and the independent replications (excluding Bem's experiments, *P*-curve analysis = 0.24) were similar. The authors report that hundreds of unpublished experiments with low *ES* would be required to annul the significant results of their meta-analysis. The authors also classified the replications into two groups: five protocols involving automatic, "fast-thinking" unconscious processing and two protocols involving "slow-thinking," deliberative processing (cf. Kahneman, 2011). All the significant results belonged to the "fast-thinking" group and the most successful one used erotic stimuli, in general agreement with the theories reviewed earlier that posit psi as a mostly nonconscious process geared to future reinforcers. The two "slow-thinking," deliberative protocols were not singly or jointly significant. Table 1 shows the cumulative results divided by categories.

In everyday life, ostensible anomalous cognition often occurs during *dreams* (Kelly & Tucker, 2015). The first comprehensive analysis of controlled studies was carried out by Yale psychologist Irvin Child (1985) on the dream psi studies conducted at the Maimonides Medical Center sleep lab. This protocol involved waking up (usually selected) participants after they had been in a REM sleep stage, which is strongly associated to dreaming, and querying them for their dream content. The task of the participant was to dream about an unknown image chosen at random by the researchers either while participants slept or at a later time. Child reported that in 20 out of 25 experiments the dream content on average had been correctly matched (blindly) to the target directly or on the top half of a binary division of multiple choices at a better than chance level, with a probability against chance of 1.46×10^{-8}. Radin (2006) estimated that the target had been judged to be on the top half of the distribution a highly significant 63% of the times (50% being mean chance expectation).

After the Maimonides program, most researchers have relied on dream diaries, which produce much poorer dream recollection than REM awakenings, rather than on studies in sleep labs, which are far more demanding. Storm et al. (2017) meta-analyzed the Maimonides and post-Maimonides studies. Table 1 includes the analysis for all and a homogeneous set, showing support of the psi hypothesis. They also report increased design rigor across time, and no association between study quality (rated blindly according to seven criteria including appropriate randomization, good masking, and so on) and *ES*. They also conducted a Bayesian analysis that confirmed their results. Their meta-analysis includes a large, well-controlled study by Watt (2014) in which independent, masked judges matched at better than chance level dream reports to the film clip that participants later saw. When alerted to a potential effect of dropouts from the study, Watt reanalyzed her data and still found a significant effect for her planned test ($p = .04$; Watt & Valášek, 2015).

RV (remote viewing) is a technique in which an individual describes a place, chosen at random, where a *sender* is located at the present or at a future time (there may also be just a location chosen without any observer there). Afterward the description is used to select the target among different possibilities. Associative RV is a type of precognitive RV in which the participant tries to guess a target to be selected in the future, and which may be associated with a particular event, for instance a change in the stock market. Table 1 shows Baptista et al.'s (2015) summary of the available data (the dataset for Milton, 1997, is homogeneous after deleting three studies). The confidence intervals of the data sets are of a similar magnitude and do not include 0.00, which would indicate no effect. The analyst for the first two data sets (Stanford Research Institute and Science Applications International Corporation; Utts, 1996) wrote that RV volunteers who had participated in previous research exhibited a greater *ES* (0.38) than novices (0.16). The psi skeptic Hyman (1995) concluded that the Science Applications International Corporation experiments were "well-designed and the investigators have taken pains to eliminate the known weaknesses in previous parapsychological research . . . I cannot provide suitable candidates for what flaws, if any, might be present." Nonetheless, objections have been raised to the Dunne and Jahn (2003) database for sampling without replacement and not always selecting the targets randomly, but even if that dataset is eliminated the overall effect remains significant (Baptista et al., 2015).

TABLES AND FIGURES

Table 1
Summary of Meta-Analytic Findings for Anomalous Cognition

Database	k (trials)	Z	p	ES	95% CI
Ganzfeld (adapted from Storm et al., 2010b)					
Combined (all)	108	8.31	$<.10^{-16}$	.142	—
Combined (hom)	102	8.13	$<.10^{-16}$	.135	[.10, .17]
New (all)	30	6.34	1.15×10^{-10}	.152	—
New (hom)	29	5.48	2.13×10^{-8}	.142	[.07, .22]
Precognition/Bem-type studies (based on Bem et al., 2015)					
Bem et al. (all)	90	6.40	1.2×10^{-10}	$.09^a$	[.06, .11]
Bem et al. (fast)	61	7.11	5.8×10^{-13}	.11	[.04, .14]
Bem et al. (slow)	29	1.38	.16	.03	[−.01, .08]
Psi dream studies (adapted from Storm et al., 2017)					
Combined (all)	52	5.01	2.72×10^{-7}	.18	—
Combined (hom)	50	5.32	5.19×10^{-8}	.20	[.11, .29]
Remote viewing (adapted from Baptista, Derakhshani, & Tressoldi, 2015; Dunne & Jahn, 2003; Milton, 1997)					
SRI	(770)			.20	[.17, .23]
SAIC	(445)			.23	[.19, .27]
Milton (hom)	75 (2,682)	5.85	2.46×10^{-9}	.17	[.10, .22]
Dunne & Jahn	88 (653)	5.42	3×10^{-8}	.21	[.18, .24]
Bierman & Rabeyron	(550)			.27	[.23, .31]
1994–2014	(314)			.39	[.14, .64]
Presentiment (adapted from Mossbridge, Tressoldi, & Utts, 2012)					
Mossbridge et al. (all)	26	5.3	5.7×10^{-8}	.21	[.13, .29]
Mossbridge et al. (hq)	13	4.4	6×10^{-6}	.24	[.13, .35]
Mossbridge et al. (lq)	13	2.96	<.002	.17	[.06, .29]
Forced choice (adapted from Baptista et al., 2015)					
Honorton/Ferrari (all)	309	11.41	6.3×10^{-25}	.020	[.09, .31]
Honorton/Ferrari (hom)	248	6.02	1.1×10^{-9}	.012	[.05, .19]
STDR (all)	91	10.82	10^{-160}	.04	—
STDR (hom)	72	4.36	6.5×10^{-66}	.01	[.01, .02]

Note. k = number of studies; Z = cumulative standard deviation from the mean; ES = mean effect size; CI = confidence interval for ES; fast = protocols involving fast-thinking processes; slow = protocols involving slow-thinking processes; hom = homogeneous; SRI = Stanford Research Institute; SAIC = Science Applications International Corporation; hq = high-quality study subset; lq = low-quality study subset; STDR = Storm, Tressoldi, and Di Risio.

Table 2
Summary of Meta-Analytic Findings for Anomalous Perturbation

Database	k (trials)	Z	p	ES	95% CI
Remote influence (adapted from Schmidt, 2015)					
EDA-DMILS (hom)	36		.001	.106	[.04, .17]
Remote staring	15		.013	.128	[.03, .23]
Attention facilitation	11		.029	.114	[.01, .22]
Noncontact healing studies (adapted from Roe, Sonnex, & Roxburgh, 2015)					
Nonhuman (all)	49		<.05	.258	[.24, .28]
Nonhuman (hq)	22		<.05	.115	[.09, .14]
Human (all)	57		<.05	.203	[.18, .23]
Human (hq)	27		<.05	.224	[.19, .25]
Dice (adapted from Radin & Ferrari, 1991)					
Radin & Ferrari (all)	73	18.2	<.001	$.0072^a$	[.0065, .0079]
Radin & Ferrari (hom)	59	3.19	.001	$.0029^a$	[.0017, .0041]
Micro-PK (adapted from Bösch, Steinkamp, & Boller, 2006)					
RNG (all)	380	2.47	<.05	$.50003^b$	
RNG (−3)	377	4.08	<.001	$.50028^b$	
Global Consciousness Project (GCP; Nelson, 2015, personal communication, 2016)					
GCP	461	7.23	2.34×10^{-13}	.33	

Note. k = number of studies; Z = cumulative standard deviation from the mean; ES = effect size; CI = confidence interval for ES; EDA = electrodermal activity; DMILS = direct mental interaction in living systems; hom = homogeneous; hq = high-quality study subset; RNG = random number generator.
[a] ES weighed by methodological quality. [b] Mean π for a binomial distribution.

Table 2. Summary of Meta-Analytic Findings for Anomalous Perturbation

In *presentiment* research, physiological activity *preceding* an unpredictable stimulus is hypothesized to anticipate the response that follows it, for instance that the preceding skin conductance to emotionally-charged stimuli will differ from that of neutral stimuli, interspersed randomly. Mossbridge, Tressoldi, and Utts (2012) meta-analyzed relevant studies published between 1978 and 2010. Table 1 shows that the overall *ES* for a physiological response preceding the stimulus was significant. The authors also conducted a masked preanalysis evaluation of the quality of the studies (according to level of peer review, type of random number generator, and whether an analysis of expectation bias had been conducted), and arrived at a division of 13 higher and 13 lower quality sets. Although both *ES*s were significant, the higher quality studies had a bigger *ES* than the lower quality ones (see Table 1). Mossbridge and collaborators (2015) later responded point-by-point to the criticisms of their meta-analysis raised by Schwarzkopf (2014).

Forced choice

In *forced-choice* studies, the guessing possibilities are finite and the possibilities are known by the person, for instance cards in a randomized deck. The protocol measures whether the participant can guess correctly more often than would be expected by chance. This was a common design in the middle of the 20th century. Honorton and Ferrari (1989) conducted a meta-analysis of forced-choice precognition research conducted between 1935 and 1987 by 62 investigators. Table 1 shows the analyses for all of 309 experiments and for the 248 homogeneous ones, revealing highly significant but very small *ES*s. They also reported that the *ES* had remained constant through the decades, that there was no relation between study outcome and an index of design quality based on eight criteria (e.g., preplanned analysis and randomization method), and that a file-drawer effect could not reasonably explain away the results. They also identified the 17 best studies, with selected samples and trial-by-trial feedback, which produced the largest effect of any other groups of studies in their database, $Z = 15.84$, $ES = 0.12$. The results of selected participants (based on prior performance) were better than those of their counterparts, $t(246) = 3.16, p = .001$ (Honorton & Ferrari, 1989, see also Baptista et al., 2015).

A second meta-analysis of forced-choice experiments was carried out by Storm, Tressoldi, and Di Risio (2012) on 91 studies conducted between 1987 and 2010, and on 72 homogeneous studies (see Table 1). They concluded that there was a small but significant effect, and no evidence that the results could be explained by low-quality designs (based on six criteria including appropriate randomization and random target positioning) or selective reporting, and that *ES*s had increased across time. Baptista et al. (2015) reported that the mean *ES* of the studies with selected participants was larger than that of unselected ones ($ES = .05$ vs. $ES = .008, p = .001$).

Anomalous perturbation

Anomalous perturbation refers to the ostensible influence of intention on nonobservable systems, evaluated statistically (there are no meta-analyses of anomalous force). *Remote influence* research evaluates the effect of intentional efforts to change a parameter in a distant living system, unmediated by known physical means. Schmidt (2015) summarized his meta-analyses of three areas: (a) *direct mental interaction in living systems*, such as measuring the electrodermal activity (EDA) of a receiver while a distant agent is, at random times, trying to make that person aroused or calm; (b) *remote staring*, or changes in the EDA of a receiver as an agent looks at him/her through video at random times from a separate room; and (c) *remote helping* (or *attention-focusing facilitation*), in which a remote helper tries at random times to help a meditator focus on a target.

Table 2 shows that all three research paradigms were supportive of psi. Schmidt (2015) wrote that the similar *ES* for the three areas validate each other and suggest the same underlying phenomenon. Nonetheless, there were some differences. The EDA–direct mental interaction in living systems dataset did not include four studies with inadequate randomization, and in the remaining 36 homogeneous studies dataset, there was a negative correlation ($r = -.40$) between *ES* and quality of study (based on 17 items including adequate randomization and preregistration). Thus, studies were weighed according to sample size and quality of the study. The remote staring dataset was homogeneous (with a nonsignificant correlation $r = .26$ between study quality and *ES*), as was the remote helping dataset, so those *ES*s were not weighed by study quality.

Noncontact healing studies include what has been called intercessory prayer, distance healing, reiki, and similar strategies that posit an effect of intention on biological tissues or whole living beings other than the person having the intention. Two previous meta-analyses on intercessory prayer, partly overlapping, came to opposite conclusions as to whether there was a valid effect (Hodge, 2007; Masters, Spielmans, & Goodson, 2006). More comprehensively, Roe, Sonnex, and Roxburgh (2015) meta-analyzed two types of studies: those relating to "nonwhole human studies" (animals, plants, and in vitro cultures) and those to "whole humans." They pointed out that whereas in the second category it would be difficult in some studies to discount the role of a placebo effect, the results for the first category were unlikely to depend on such mechanisms as unconditioned expectancies.

For the nonwhole human studies, Roe et al. (2015) identified 49 heterogeneous studies, which had a significant weighted *ES*. Weighing was carried out without awareness of results or authorship and included such variables as treatment allocation randomization and good masking procedures. Because there were negative correlations between indices of experimental quality and *ES*, the authors selected the 22 studies rated as having good designs. Although the *ES* diminished, it remained significant (see Table 2). For research on humans, the authors identified 57 studies with adequate methodology, which produced a significant result (see Table 2), but because there was a negative correlation between design quality and *ES*, they analyzed the 27 studies with better methodology, and the *ES* remained significant (see Table 2). Roe et al. warned that because the funnel plot of the *ES*s suggest publication bias (and some authors did not provide exact probability values when not significant), results should be taken cautiously.

Dice

Trying to affect the fall of dice, typically in a machine to avoid possible manipulation, was a common research paradigm used in the mid-20th century. Radin and Ferrari (1991) meta-analyzed 148 studies involving more than 2 million dice throws, in which participants intended to affect the fall of dice without touching them, and which produced a highly significant but small effect in the expected direction ($Z = 19.68$; $p < .01$), with Z values decreasing and methodological quality improving over time. This dataset includes studies with a physical bias of using higher dice faces as targets, so Table 2 shows significant but very small results for 73 studies after controlling for this artifact, as well as for a homogenized set of 59 studies, indicating that the dice fell more often on the face intended than would be expected by chance. For the homogenized dataset, *ES* did not relate to design quality. In comparison, in the 31 control studies the selected face did not fall more often than would be expected by chance, $Z = 0.36$, $p > .05$.

Micro-PK

Bösch, Steinkamp, and Boller (2006) meta-analyzed 380 studies on attempts to affect random number generators (RNGs). Table 2 shows significant but very small effects for a random-effects model on a dataset including and excluding the three largest studies. Although the 137 control studies in which there was no intention to affect the RNGs did not show a significant deviation, $Z = -1.51$, $p = .13$, the authors concluded that the results might be explained by publication bias because there was great heretogeneity and fewer studies below $p < .05$ and $p < .01$ levels than would be expected by chance. In a later reanalysis of the Bösch et al. data, Varvoglis and Bancel (2015, p. 274) concurred that the distribution of significance levels suggested some publication bias, but posited that an "extremely large" and unrealistic file drawer effect would be required to annul the results. They proposed instead that the data heterogeneity could be explained by the talent (methodological and perhaps parapsychological) of particular experimenters and the far better than average performance of two participants in the PEAR (Princeton Engineering Anomalies Research) dataset, who contributed a quarter of the data with zs of 5.6 and 3.4 as compared with 0.8 for the remaining participants.

In *implicit anomalous perturbation,* the experimenter sets hidden or secondary RNGs to be influenced by participants without any necessary conscious intent. These studies partially inspired a research program, having been conducted now for more than 15 years, known as The Global Consciousness Project (Nelson, 2015). Its premise is that events that simultaneously impact many people throughout the world (e.g., the 9/11 attacks) create a coherence in human consciousness that affects the randomness of a network of 65 RNGs located in various countries. The collective RNG output from a time window around such major events is compared with times in which no such events occur. Table 2 shows the analysis of 461 events, with a significant result and a sizable *ES* at the level of the event (Nelson, 2015, and personal communication, 2016). By their nature, these data come from a single source, but data and analyses are accessible at noosphere.princeton.edu/results.html#alldata.

Comparing all of these meta-analyses, there are consistent patterns. First, overall the meta-analyses have been supportive of the psi hypothesis, with those that have not (e.g., Galak et al., 2012; Milton & Wiseman, 1999) generally superseded by alternative, more comprehensive meta-analyses. Second, the analyses relating to *free-response* paradigms have the highest *ES*s, ranging from 0.11 to 0.39, with most over 0.2. Then follow *ES*s for *remote, noncontact influence*, ranging from 0.10 to 0.26. The *ES*s for *forced-choice* research, ranging from 0.01 to 0.04, are about one order of magnitude smaller and the anomalous perturbation *ES*s for *dice* and *micro-PK* (excluding the Global Consciousness Project) are also very small. Third, selected participants seem to evidence more psi than nonselected ones.

With respect to the last point, the most consistent data sets (ganzfeld, dream studies, and RV) have often used selected participants, and the analyses reviewed earlier for ganzfeld, forced choice, and micro-PK strongly support this practice (for research with "gifted" individuals under controlled conditions, see Edge, Morris, Palmer, & Rush, 1986). Characteristics shown to increase the likelihood of performing well in a psi experiment include a belief that one will do well in the study, some psychological traits (e.g., extraversion and openness to experience), a mental practice such as meditation, and previous experience in a psi experiment (for a review, see Cardeña & Marcusson-Clavertz, 2015). In a recent meta-analysis on forced-choice experiments, performance correlated positively with belief in psi, $r = .13$, $p = .002$, extraversion, $r = .08$, $p = .02$, and openness to experience, $r = .12$, $p = .02$ (Zdrenka & Wilson, 2017). Artists tend to score better than chance and other groups (Holt, Delanoy, & Roe, 2004).

There is evidence that testing while a participant is in a different state of consciousness than the ordinary, waking one is conducive to psi performance. Two of the more successful paradigms involve naturally occurring or induced alterations (i.e., ganzfeld, dreaming). In an earlier review, Honorton (1977) compared performance in psi studies involving hypnosis, meditation, induced relaxation, and ganzfeld and concluded that they produced better results than would be expected by chance, ranging from 1.2×10^{-9} to 6×10^{-12} (for more recent reviews, see Cardeña et al., 2015). Storm et al. (2010b, p. 476) compared research with ganzfeld, other purported psi-enhancing techniques such as meditation, and those not using psi-enhancing techniques. Ganzfeld had the largest ES (0.14), followed by other enhancing techniques ($ES = 0.11$) and studies without techniques ($ES = -0.03$), the last one differing from ganzfeld (ES mean difference $= 0.17$, $p = .005$). The effect of ganzfeld may be mediated by how much it alters the state of consciousness (Marcusson-Clavertz & Cardeña, 2011; Roe, Hodrien, & Kirkwood, 2012).

Discussion

This overview of meta-analyses of various different research protocols supports the psi hypothesis. The analyses satisfy the "local and global criteria" specified by a critic of psi who demanded replicability, consistency of effects, and cumulativeness (Office of Technology Assessment, 1989). The meta-analyses, conducted on studies using different protocols and by different researchers, provide cumulative vertical and horizontal support of psi. Vertical in the sense that across time different protocols have continued to produce positive results beyond what would be expected by chance, and with increasing methodological rigor; horizontal in the sense that there is support for psi across research areas. If only one or a few protocols out of 10 were significant and the rest were not, it would be easier to speculate that the supportive results might be due to an artifact. In addition, the rigor of the psi meta-analyses has increased with time and typically include evaluation of possible selective reporting, quality of studies, and so on. The article will now consider some common criticisms of psi.

If psi phenomena are real, why do not all studies replicate them?

Considering the small *ES* found and potential sources of variability, including psychological and perhaps parapsychological experimenter effects (Palmer & Millar, 2015), one *should* expect some studies not to replicate (cf. Barrett, 2015; Lewontin, 1994). As Harvard professor Robert Rosenthal (1990) opined, given the levels of statistical power at which we normally operate, we have no right to expect the proportion of significant results that we typically do expect, even if in nature there is a very real and very important effect. (Utts, 1991)

Appendix C
How we Know Consciousness is not on the Electromagnetic Spectrum but Can Readily Engage with it

The most obvious reason that the fundamental consciousness field cannot be electromagnetic in nature is that, if it were, and given its omnipresence, we would be detecting it constantly, both perceptually and instrumentally, instead of only rarely. We notice electromagnetic effects secondarily, when a conscious agent chooses to engage with the electromagnetic spectrum, for example when lights flicker in a séance room, an EMF meter registers a signal, or a UAP suddenly disables a vehicle's electrical system. That intent is required for consciousness to manifest electromagnetically shows that it is not itself *made* of electrons, nor is it the same thing as the fundamental quantum field that produces electrons.

Intent can be considered broadly, also, to include changes that affect electromagnetism only incidentally, as when a conscious agent lowers its frequency for some other purpose and, in so doing, crosses down through the frequency range of the electromagnetic spectrum. Indeed, such interference is hardly avoidable—whether or not we earthlings happen to notice it in any given case—because this energy, on the OM side of the ledger, is the very glue that binds atoms and molecules together and thus makes matter itself, *our world itself*, possible. If you are a visiting spirit, you can't help but tangle with electricity, so you might as well use it to communicate or to get something done if possible.

Often, it's not possible. In both daylight and artificial light, the photon stream typically overwhelms and preempts any subtle spiritual energies attempting to come through, which is why darkness tends to be a prerequisite for successful séances. In other circumstances, too, electricity can block contact, again attesting to the independence of this force from the fundamental consciousness field. During a séance in London on the evening of July 26, 1868, speaking through an entranced D. D. Home, a spirit explained that

> We are entirely dependent upon atmospheric conditions. Now, tonight, the atmosphere is so surcharged with electricity that it appears to us quite thick, like sand. It is so unlike our own that it is almost impossible for us to get near you. We feel like men wading through a quicksand—slipping back as fast as we advance. At other times, when your earthly atmosphere is in a natural state, it is more like our own, and we have no difficulty in being near you.[1]

Taking a far more traditionally scientific approach, others have experimentally demonstrated the difference between consciousness and electromagnetism.

Barriers and distance

In *The Nature of Mind: Parapsychology and the Role of Consciousness in the Physical World* (2014), Douglas M. Stokes lays out objections to any theory seeking to explain psi (psychic/spiritual phenomena) within an electromagnetic context. Here's an excerpt.

> One of the earliest proponents of an electromagnetic theory of psi (psychic/spiritual phenomena) was Joseph Glanvill (1636-1660), a contemporary of Newton, who proposed that telepathic exchanges were caused by the vibrations of the "ether" (see Jaki, 1969). More modern proponents of electromagnetic theories of psi include Kazhinsky (1962); Becker (1990, 1992); MacLellan (1997); and Vasilescu and Vasilescu (1996, 2001).
>
> Severe difficulties confront any attempt to explain psi phenomena on the basis of electromagnetic waves. These include the apparent ability of psi signals to penetrate barriers normally impervious to electromagnetic radiation; the apparent failure of psi phenomena to obey the usual inverse-square law governing the falloff in electromagnetic effects with distance; the feeble strength of the electromagnetic signals emanating from the brain compared to the power that would be required to

send a telepathic signal or perform a psychokinetic feat over any reasonable distance; and the lack of any plausible neurological mechanism whereby such a signal could be encoded, generated, received, and decoded. Each of these difficulties will be discussed in turn.

Barrier Experiments. Successful telepathy experiments have been reported in which the subjects were electromagnetically shielded from one another by Faraday cages and other types of barriers, ruling out the exchange of most electromagnetic signals (e.g., Vasiliev, 1976; Targ & Puthoff,1977; Ullman & Krippner, 1969).

Distance Independence. If ESP and PK effects were due to electromagnetic waves transmitted between the subject and the target person or object, it would be expected that psi success would decrease with increasing distance between the subject and target (as the intensity of electromagnetic information emitted from a point source is inversely proportional to the square of the distance from the point). The small electrical power of the brain (discussed in the next section), combined with the inverse square law for electromagnetic radiation, would seem to imply that psi effects could not occur over large distances if they were due to electromagnetic radiation. However, successful remote viewing experiments have been conducted with the percipient (viewer) in Detroit and the agent (sender) in Italy (Schlitz and Gruber, 1980, 1981). A series of successful PK experiments, with distances ranging from 10 miles to 1,100 miles separating the PK agent from the target apparatus, have been reported by Tedder and his associates (Tedder & Monty, 1981; Tedder & Braud, 1981; Tedder and Bloor, 1982). Nelson, Dunne, Dobyns and Jahn (1996) and Jahn and Dunne (2005) report that the size of the PK and remote viewing effects obtained by the Princeton Engineering Anomalies Research (PEAR) team were independent of the spacetime separations between the subjects and the target. Many more examples could be cited.

The apparent lack of dependence of psi effects on spatial and temporal proximity is evidence not only against electromagnetic theories of psi, but against all theories of psi based on known or currently postulated physical signals. Indeed, the lack of dependence of psi on spacetime proximity was one of the factors that led J. B. Rhine, the founder of experimental parapsychology, to proclaim that psi phenomena indicate that the mind has a nonphysical component. Thus, psi phenomena have long been regarded as evidence against physicalist theories of mind. The physicalistic metaphysics underlying current orthodox scientific theories may explain why the debate over the existence of psi has been so heated and why the evidence for psi phenomena is so strongly rejected by the scientific establishment. In this regard, one might recall the comments of Anthony Freeman, the Editor of the *Journal of Consciousness Studies*, who recently noted that "orthodox science is orthodox religion's true heir" (Freeman, 2005, p. 6).

"Signal" theories of psi are all based on the assumption that some relatively localized particle or wave carries the psi message. As we have seen, these theories all have rather severe drawbacks. However, experiments in the quantum mechanical realm indicate that the universe does not consist exclusively of discrete, mutually isolated and localized particles and objects. In fact, quantum wave theory paints a picture of the universe that is not at all hostile to psi phenomena. Indeed, the principle of nonlocality in quantum mechanics would almost lead one to *anticipate* the existence of psi. If not even two protons separated by light-years can be conceptualized as separate objects, perhaps it is also incorrect to consider persons as encapsulated, spatially isolated entities. Seemingly separate persons may in fact merely be different facets of a higher nonlocal entity. The mysterious connections between apparently isolated elementary particles in the field of quantum mechanics make the prospect of psi interactions between people much more palatable.[2]

Extremely low frequency?
The Psi Encyclopedia delves into the effort to salvage the electromagnetism explanation by appeal to the very edge of the spectrum.

> Russian physiologist and psychologist Leonid Leonidovich Vasiliev (1891-1966) was the first person to seriously ask the question, Is nonlocal perception an electromagnetic phenomenon? In 1932, his institute received an assignment from the Soviet government "to initiate an experimental study of telepathy with the aim of determining as far as possible its physical basis: What is the wavelength of electromagnetic radiation that produces 'mental radio,' the transmission of information from one brain to another, if such a transmission exists?"
>
> Vasiliev looked at what today would be described as nonlocal perception and perturbation (PK), although he didn't use those terms. He would ask participants to focus on a target individual and to stimulate them in some way. He found that it worked. He would put people into caves or mine shafts in Faraday cages so that the participants were shielded from most of EM radiation and ask them to write down images or letters. To his very considerable surprise, Vasiliev found that neither distance nor shielding made any difference in the quality of the nonlocal perception. By changing the shielding, he finally concluded that if nonlocal perception were electromagnetic it could only be in the range of Extreme Low Frequency (ELF) (1-300Hrtz) signaling because he had eliminated everything else. The only way to test that, to shield from ELF, would be to submerge the participant in the sea at a depth ELF could not penetrate, and then to see if they could still successfully

complete an experiment requiring nonlocal perception. But that required a submarine, and Vasiliev, despite all his efforts, could not set up such an experiment.

Stephan Schwartz, then the Special Assistant for Research and Analysis to the Chief of Naval Operations, became familiar with Vasiliev's research in 1971 and saw it in the context of the remote viewing research he had done earlier; he decided to do the experiment and tried to interest the Navy in doing it, but like Vasiliev he was unsuccessful.

Contemporaneously, the Navy had decided that ELF, precisely because it will penetrate at least some depth of seawater, could be a means to communicate with the service's deep ocean ballistic missile submarines. They wanted the boats to stay as deeply submerged as possible so that Soviet satellites would not detect the heat bloom from the sub's nuclear reactor, and thus be able to locate and track it. In their Project Sanguine, they explored the ELF-seawater relationship with meticulous care and discovered that the bit rate of transmission using ELF was restricted to just a few numbers, since frequency also dictates the amount of information that can be transmitted.

Thanks to Project Sanguine, Schwartz finally had the piece of the puzzle that Vasiliev had lacked. He understood even before conducting the experiment that the amount of data routinely provided in a remote viewing session far exceeded the transmission bit rate of ELF. With ELF, the maximum bit rate dB/dt is equal to somewhat less than half the frequency. A single letter, given an alphabet of 26 symbols, requires 4.7 bits (since $2^{4.7} = 26$). So, a 5-letter word requires about 24 bits. In contrast, it has been calculated that a single visual observation requires about 100 bits of data, and a simple geometric form about 60 bits. In practical terms, this data transmission restriction supported the idea that nonlocal perception was not an electromagnetic process. But doing the actual experiment was, of course, indispensable.[3]

Project Deep Quest

In 1976, through the auspices of the Institute for Marine and Coastal Studies of the University of Southern California, and the generosity of its directors Don Walsh and Don Keach—retired naval officers internationally recognized for their deep ocean engineering expertise—Stephan Schwartz was given the temporary use of a research submersible, Taurus, and created Project Deep Quest. This had three parts: 1. Ascertain whether the ELF hypothesis was viable; 2. Use well-established remote viewing protocol to see if a reliable communications channel could be established; 3. Find out whether, by using remote viewing, a previously unknown wreck on or under the seafloor could be located and described in detail.

Because Taurus had a 1,200-foot depth limit, the ELF portion of the experiment could not be definitive; to get sufficient shielding for that would require a submersible with at least a 6,000-foot depth limit. However, by placing the submarine at depth, which highly attenuated the signal and further reducing the bit rate, along with the viewer being at over five hundred miles distance from the outbound target, a functionally definitive experiment could be carried out.

The Deep Quest fieldwork with Taurus was carried out over three days in June 1977. It showed that ELF was a highly improbable explanation for nonlocal perception, that remote viewing could be used to send a message and, equally important, by means of remote viewing, a previously unknown shipwreck off Santa Catalina Island, an area already surveyed by a variety of electronic technologies, was located and accurately reconstructed in detail.[4]

See the short documentary "Project Deep Quest" on the Nemoseen Media YouTube channel and the interview on the New Thinking Allowed channel, "Project Deep Quest with Stephan A. Schwartz."

Psychokinesis (PK)

Not only is the informational access that operates in telepathy and remote viewing distinct from the electromagnetic spectrum, it turns out that so are the physical changes introduced in micro- or macro-PK. No electromagnetic influence was associated with the exhaustive, twenty-eight-year-long random event generator experiments at Princeton's PEAR lab, and in their peer-reviewed study on Ariel Farias's ability to partially levitate tables, Gimeno and Burgo tested for this natural force as well and reported categorically, "No variations of electric and magnetic fields were found to be associated with the phenomena."[5]

This is because behind all psychic/spiritual (psi) phenomena is the fundamental consciousness field—counterpart to, and collaborator with, the fluidlike quantum fields that give rise to all OM/energy—and, again, the fundamental consciousness field is independent of the field that produces electrons. However, myriad examples exist of electromagnetic side effects associated with psi phenomena. Their consistency and strength suggest that the two fields must be vibrationally highly compatible.

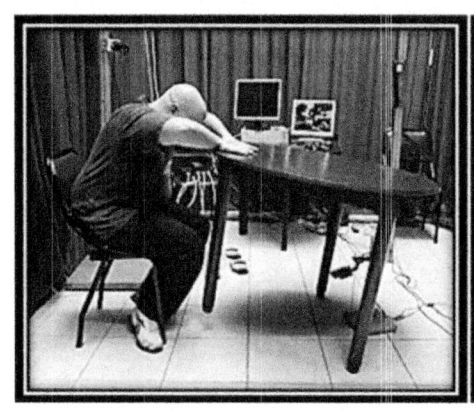

Electromagnetism, technology, and spirit signals

> *In concentrating the mind on any one spirit person, you are sending out real, live, active forces. These forces pass through the air in precisely the same way [though using a different form of energy] as electric waves do, and they never miss their mark. You*

> *concentrate on Mr. A. in the spirit world, and immediately Mr. A. is conscious of a force coming to him.*
>
> —William Stead, *The Blue Island*

However the conversion works between the energy source of the fundamental consciousness field and that of the universal field that gives rise to electrons, one thing is crystal clear: It does work, and to powerful effect.

One of Thomas Edison's (1847-1931) little-known ambitions was to build a device through which to hear the voices of the dead, according to a nearly lost chapter of the inventor's memoirs. He wanted to create a sort of "spirit phone" that recorded the utterances of departed souls. This chapter was expunged from English-language editions of his book until many years after his death.[6]

Nikola Tesla (1856-1943) tried to beat Edison to the breakthrough with a crystal radio receiver. In 1901, he wrote in his journal, "My first observations positively terrified me, as there was present in them something mysterious, not to say supernatural, and I was alone in my laboratory at night." In 1918, after tinkering with a new version of the receiver, he wrote, "The sounds I am listening to every night appear to be human voices conversing back and forth in a language I cannot understand."[7] There was no radio station near him, and ham radio networks did not yet exist.

It makes sense to reach out by means of a communication device. "Radios and telephones are already direct voice communication devices," writes Steve Parsons, physicist, member of the Society for Psychical Research, and paranormal investigator for the past forty years. "If connections could take place," he continues, "those would be the most obvious and likely methods to be employed. When, for example, the SETI project astronomers and scientists were looking for evidence of alien life forms, they also turned to radio communications and electromagnetic emissions as the most probable and likely area to look for evidence."[8]

By the same token, there's powerful evidence, too, that spirits engage in their own concerted efforts, making use of the electromagnetic spectrum to reach back to Earth. In *The Source and Significance of Coincidences*, Sharon Hewitt Rawlette documents several representative examples of spirits using common electronics as their go-to mode of contact. It's important to mention that a spirit need not understand the complex inner workings of a phone, say, in order to send a message through it. Those still living on Earth don't either; the phone itself knows how to function, and the goal-oriented intent of the user engages the system.

A hospice patient named Mary Esther had just passed away, and the nurses were attempting to notify her son, but his phone line was constantly busy. While her doctor was at the nurses' station asking for an update on their attempts, the phone rang. The caller ID said the call was coming from Mary Esther's room. A nurse answered and obviously heard something that dismayed her, because she passed the phone to the doctor.

> He reports hearing a lot of static and a far-away voice saying, "Tell my son I'm okay. Tell my son I'm okay." It sounded just like Mary Esther. Of course, they rushed into her room, but there was no one there besides her cold body. Thirty minutes later, Mary Esther's son arrived at the hospital. He reported that he, too, had received a phone call from his mother at a time he now knew to have been after her death. She'd told him over and over, "I am okay. I love you. Don't worry about me. I'm okay." Someone wanting to play devil's advocate could argue that the living person's memories, combined with their strong wish to hear from their loved one, might be capable of manifesting a phone call. But in the above case, the calls came to more than one person from the same deceased personality at approximately the same time. Dr. Lerma and the nurse heard the same voice, and there is no reason to think that they were particularly wishing for after-death contact with Mary Esther, whom they only knew in a professional capacity.

* * *

Joe Dioca's wife died suddenly just six days after he'd undergone a heart procedure. A week and a half after her death, but still five days before his follow-up appointment, he got a call from his doctor's office. The receptionist told him that they were going to move his

UAPs and the Afterlife 159

appointment up to the following morning because his wife had left them a voicemail saying he didn't look good and needed to be seen sooner. The following day, it was discovered that he was experiencing life-threatening arrythmia requiring immediate treatment.

* * *

A young man had recently survived a tragic car accident in which a friend of his died. Two weeks after the death, the mother got a phone call from someone she recognized as her son's deceased friend. The friend seemed panicky and was asking to speak to her son. He said, "Hurry, put him on, please, I don't understand what's going on. It's like the world is turning bizarre.."[9]

"The messages sent on your telephones require less effort," Rawlette quotes a spirit as reporting, "because your thoughts alone are enough to put the message onto your telephone. Your telephones themselves already have an energy that we use to communicate with you."[9] In other words, it seems, thought and electromagnetic energy have an intimate relationship.

There are many more such cases chronicled in Rogo and Bayless's *Phone Calls from the Dead*, but all such spontaeneous telephone contacts comprise only a small slice of a much broader area of systematic study involving electricity and the "departed." Insstrumental Transcommunication (ITC) has a rich and impressive history within psychical research. You'll probably have heard frequent references to EVP (electronic voice phenomena) in mainstream media, but despite its popularity, especially on sensationalistic "ghost hunter" TV shows, it is true that spirits do sometimes communicate in this way. In 1959, for instance, the Swedish painter and film producer Friedrich Jürgenson had recorded bird songs. Replaying the tape later, he heard his dead father's voice and then the spirit of his deceased wife calling his name, whereupon he commenced his decades-long investigation of ITC.

You can learn about ITC in depth from Daniel Drasin's documentary "Calling Earth" and from these trailblazing books: *Voice Transmissions with the Deceased* (1967) by Friedrich Jürgenson; *Breakthrough* (1971) by Konstantin Raudive; *Listen! New Discoveries about the Afterlife: Scientific Research on Contact with the Invisible* (2017) by Anna Maria Wauters and Hans Otto Koenig; and Anabela Cardoso's excellent series of books, most recently *Electronic Contact with the Dead: What do the Voices Tell Us?* (2017). Cardoso explains the ITC process, results, and significance very accessibly, too, in YouTube videos including "Learning from the Voices of Instrumental Transcommunication with Anabela Cardoso," "Anabela Cardoso's Electronic Contacts with the Beyond," and others on her eponymous channel.

I'll share just one passage from the voluminous records of Konstantin Raudive (1909-1974) because it harmonizes so well with our recognition of the ubiquity and immanence of information in the fundamental consciousness field. Raudive writes,

> Once again, I noticed the characteristic peculiarities of the phenomenon. Sentences are compressed, the meaning is usually obscure, and in all languages used, grammatical rules are ignored; for instance, the German word *binde* ("bind") becomes "bindu", a combination of *bind* and du, the German word for "thou." Neologisms are particularly remarkable.
>
> My question [one day] as to how it had been known that [I had just switched on the recorder] was answered by a woman's voice: "Wir waren in deinem Zimmer." (24g: 041)—German: "We were in your room." Sentences in Latvian and Russian followed, for example: "Izrādās tāds nevīzīgs, nebo!"—literally, "It becomes apparent that he is negligent, oh Heaven!" but as we might say, "Heavens, he's obviously been careless!"
>
> The next sentence is striking: "Jundahl kan gå själv,— oh vecā pott! Bindu han an de(m) mort-bed!" (24g: 041) The sentence is composed of five languages: *Jundahl*—a name; *kan gå själv*—Swedish: *vecā*— Latvian; *pott*—North German dialect or Swedish; *bindu*—modified German; *han*—Swedish; *an de(m)*— German; *mort*—Latin or one of the Romance languages; *bed*—English. In English the sentence would run: "Jundahl can walk by himself, the old pot. Tie him to the death-bed." In this context, yet another

sentence became audible: "Lido ernst nach ziami auf Konstant! Konstantin, Alex." (24g: 042) This is a mixture of Latvian and German words: *lido*—Latvian: flying; *ernst*—German: serious; *nach*—German: to; *ziami*—Latvian: Earth; *auf*—German: on (or: to) can be understood in English as: "Fly in earnest to Earth to Konstant! Konstantin, Alex!"

The voices speak in six different languages, often several in a single sentence, the experimenter or his collaborators are often addressed by name, and the voices repeatedly mention their own names and allude to situations in their past Earthly lives which are quite unknown to those present.[10]

This exquisite potpourri displays once again the encompassing fertility and specificity of the fundamental consciousness field.

A possible conversion process

> The spirits at Scole explained that they were not working with electricity as we know it but with an analogue form of energy that is common in their realm. "Don't fall into the misunderstanding that we are dealing with electromagnetic waves because we are not."[11]

We must infer some efficient energy-conversion process between the form used by the fundamental consciousness field and that of the fundamental quantum field that births electrons. But how might this work? It turns out there's a tricky customer who's just like an electron but 207 times heavier; it has been called a "super electron." It blinks in and out of existence in 2.2 millionths of a second. It's called the *muon*. Like IM, muons are around us all the time, and their behavior doesn't exactly play by the rules.

In 2021, the Fermilab near Chicago confirmed a strange result from twenty years earlier. Alex Keshavarzi, researcher in particle physics at the University of Manchester, writes that the Fermilab put muons in a vertical magnetic field that makes them twirl horizontally like little compass needles. The experiment involves measuring to exquisite precision the rate at which the muons twirl. The frequency at which they twirl reveals how magnetic [energetic] they are, which in principle can point to new particles.[12]

This frequency can point to new particles because the intensity of the wobble indicates the level of energy that's influencing the muons, and more is striking and energizing them than can be accounted for within the Standard Model of physics. Some have hailed this result as revealing nothing short of "a new force of nature," a fifth force beyond the traditional four. A "new force" and a "new particle" are equivalent; $E = MC^2$ means that energy and mass (matter) are interchangeable, different forms of the same thing.

The experiment at Fermilab measured muons' higher-than-expected frequency within a powerful electromagnetic field, but what it revealed speaks to their intrinsic nature whatever their surroundings. Something beyond current understanding is "exciting" them, that is, raising their energy level, aka "bumping" them. They become a force carrier, which in quantum field theory is also known as a *messenger particle, intermediate particle*, or *exchange particle*.

"The find," Keshavarzi explains, "suggests that there are new particles or forces that aren't part of our globally accepted theory, interacting with the muons and causing them to wobble faster. It's the closest glimpse we've had."[13]

So, what are we beginning to glimpse here? What's the secret source of this extra power boost? Nobody knows, of course, but if indeed it's spirit matter/energy at play, then what we're likely looking at is the—or *one* of the—means by which energy is converted between reality's higher-frequency and its lower-frequency conditions, how spirits are able to flicker our lights, turn appliances off and on, ring our phones, and cause bright orbs to fly through séance rooms. They'd be sending countless tiny charges through these higher-vibrational super electrons down to our ordinary electrons, contributing fresh juice—like pulling a thermodynamic rabbit out of a hat.

Forms of scrying

> *The word* scry *comes from* descry, *which means "to detect something by looking, or catch sight of something." It is a method of contact with the spirit realm by means of a medium such as glass, crystal, smoke, mirror, water, fire, sound, etc.*
>
> *The evidence of scrying is global and millennia old. There is documented use of scrying all the way back to ancient Babylonia (around 1800 BCE).*
> —BackyardBanshee.com
>
> *The souls here try very hard to reach the people they knew. But hundreds simply never get through because those they are trying to reach don't know that it's really possible to talk to us. It can be very frustrating.*
> —Martin and Romanowski, *Love Beyond Life*
>
> *The way in which I receive information is as much about the skill set of the discarnate as it is about me. I am like an instrument. One soul may be able to play Beethoven while another may only be able to play 'Chopsticks.'"*
> —Julie Beischel, *From the Mouths of Mediums*

Remarkably, ITC through a radio can succeed *even when the receiver is removed*; in such cases, of course, the communicator is not making use of the electromagnetic spectrum but rather the white noise or static itself. Contact by means of electricity, though prevalent, is but a subset of the wider category of *scrying*, and scrying is just our little name for the primordial interplay of fundamental IM and OM fields when a spirit is trying to get in touch.

Although some are able to manifest directly before our eyes and ears, others need help, a more concrete medium to work with in making their presence known, something denser than they are that they can get a grip or traction on and manipulate with their own PK. Even vapor is far denser than spirit substance, and those water droplets are every bit as readymade for intelligent control as electrons.

Brazilian afterlife researcher Sonia Rinaldi, for example, famously employs steam, mist, smoke, light-and-shadow, running water, etc., to connect people with their loved ones. The idea is that beloved spirits are often *right here*, sharing the same space with us but lacking a feasible means of outreach. I recommend the documentary "Rinaldi: Instrumental Trans-Communication to the Other Side" and the video "Sonia Rinaldi presents 'Images from the Afterlife' 7 June 2020" on the We Don't Die Radio channel.

References

1. Windham Thomas Wyndham-Quin Adare, *Experiences in Spiritualism with D. D. Home*, London: 1886.
2. Douglas M. Stokes, *The Nature of Mind: Parapsychology and the Role of Consciousness in the Physical World* (2014)
3. *Psi Encyclopedia.* https://psi-encyclopedia.spr.ac.uk/articles/remote-viewing
4. Ibid.
5. Juan Gimeno and Dario Burgo, "Laboratory Research on a Presumably PK-Gifted Subject," *Journal of Scientific Exploration* Vol. 31, No. 2, 2017.
6. "Thomas Edison's 'lost' idea: A device to hear the dead," Phys.org, 2015.
7. Michele Debczak, Mentalfloss.com, 2019.
8. Biju Belinky, "Ghost in the machine: inside the internet's paranormal history," Huckmag.com, 2019.
9. Sharon Hewitt Rawlette, *The Source and Significance of Coincidences*, published independently: 2019.
10. Konstantin Raudive, *Listen! New Discoveries about the Afterlife: Scientific Research on Contact with the Invisible*, Taplinger Publishing Company, New York: 2017.
11. From the documentary "Scole: The Afterlife Experiment" by Daniel Drasin
12. Science 2021 www.science.org/content/article/particle-mystery-deepens-physicists-confirm-muon-more-magnetic-predicted
13. "Muon physics: Have we found a new force of nature? | Alex Keshavarzi | TEDxManchester"

Appendix D
Qi and Spirit

In section 4.9, I said there's no such thing as OM without IM. This is true, but the reverse is not. The term OM is just shorthand to distinguish it qualitatively from IM, but in fact all OM is *hybrid* matter, primordially synthesized with IM. IM can also, however, operate on its own in pure form as consciousness, unencumbered by OM. In this form, it can both *know* OM (physical information), as in remote viewing, and *act upon* it, as in PK. This appendix will focus upon IM in its pure form.

Qi

Here in the West, there is no reliable scientific evidence for the subtle energy variously known as *qi*, *prana*, *ka*, *ruh*, etc. This is because researchers have assumed it's a form of electromagnetism, but as I demonstrated in Appendix C, the fundamental consciousness field is not on the electromagnetic spectrum and is not to be confused with the OM quantum fields; instead, it is its own autonomous field that can interact with OM fields.

Let me start with examples from *qigong*, a skill cultivated through long practice that harnesses qi through movement and intention setting. In the video "Chi master puts animals to sleep" on the DeskNews.com channel, qigong master Kanzawa Sensei causes a group of alpacas—never trained for this—to sink to their knees in the middle of the afternoon, even laying their long necks on the dirt. He demonstrates that the process works better the farther away he stands from the animals; other forms of energy dissipate with distance, but the flow of information—"lie down!"—does not. Distant energy healing, too, also known as remote healing, has been practiced in the East for centuries by qigong masters and by their alternatively titled counterparts outside of China and Japan.

Just as remote viewing and telepathy are entirely unaffected even by vast distances, qi energy functions independently of the constraints of spacetime. Not surprisingly, then, qigong is also a close cousin to psychokinesis. Loyd Auerbach, author of *Mind Over Matter* and many other books, shares a personal example of distant influence in "Psychokinesis (PK) with Loyd Auerbach" on the New Thinking Allowed channel.

> There was a martial artist named Guy Savelli. Among the things he claimed he could do was to push someone at a distance. One of the tests we did was for him to influence a subject while watching them on a video camera from an isolation room. He was given random movement assignments, to make the subject move forward, backward, or side to side. I was that subject. At one point, he was asked to push me backward several times in a row. I almost fell over. I felt someone shoving me.

Later in the interview, host Jeffrey Mishlove relates that he sponsored Uri Geller's first major public appearance in the United States in 1973, at UC Berkely.

> At the time, I had a radio program on KPFA and brought Uri on the show, and we began getting calls from the audience reporting spoons bending spontaneously in their homes, and watches that hadn't worked for years started running again. We got dozens and dozens of calls.

In other words, the ubiquitous fluid of consciousness can *inform* objects—persuade them to change form—in many ways, none of which employs mechanical or electromagnetic force. In this context, we remember Dean Radin's assessment of his own spoon-bending success.

> It's not imposing anything from the outside, it's doing something that happens way down deep at the microscopic scale and changes the information

> structure from the inside. Everything is saturated with energy all the time. All you need to do is essentially to turn a switch in the right way and the energy is released.

Though mimicking direct OM-to-OM contact, PK effects depend instead on a direct relationship between conscious intent and result, on the energetic kinship between them, on the same principle plied by qigong masters, reiki healers, remote viewers, mind-readers, and—surprise surprise—by mediums in touch with spirits. Spirits are nothing more or less than consciousness.

The subtle body

> *"There is a natural body, and there is a spiritual body." Those words have fallen from the lips of priests, over the bodies of the so-called dead, for thousands of years, yet not a single minister who uttered them, nor one among the millions of mourners, who for centuries past heard them, ever formed any rational conception of what they meant—and for ages the world has been filled with sorrow.*
> —Edward C. Randall, *The French Revelation*

In keeping with the elegant economy of nature, the very same fundamentals that allow for the above manifestations are also behind immortality itself. And just as we can play in the fundamental consciousness field while embodied here on Earth, we can also swim free of the body at times, enjoying a full dress rehearsal for the ultimate release called death.

In 1958, Robert Monroe, a radio broadcasting executive, began experiencing unwelcome sensations, all-over vibrations and paralysis accompanied by a bright light that appeared to be shining on him from a shallow angle. Visits to his doctor turned up nothing, and so Monroe decided he had no choice but to simply allow the symptoms to play out, to develop as they may.

> It was late at night, and I was lying in bed before sleep. My wife had fallen asleep beside me. There was a surge that seemed to be in my head, and quickly the condition spread through my body. As I lay there

trying to decide how to analyze the thing, I just happened to think how nice it would be to take a glider up and fly the next afternoon (my hobby at that time). Without considering any consequences—not knowing there would be any—I thought of the pleasure it would bring.

After a moment, I became aware of something pressing against my shoulder. Half-curious, I reached back and up to feel what it was. My hand encountered a smooth wall. I moved my hand along the wall the length of my arm, and it continued smooth and unbroken. My senses fully alert, I tried to see in the dim light. It was a wall, and I was lying against it with my shoulder. I immediately reasoned that I had gone to sleep and fallen out of bed. Then I looked again. Something was wrong. This wall had no windows, no furniture against it, no doors, and there was a strange fountain coming out of it. It was not a wall in my bedroom. Yet somehow it was familiar. Identification came instantly. It wasn't a wall, it was the ceiling. I was floating against the ceiling, bouncing gently with any movement I made. I rolled in the air, startled, saw that the "fountain" was actually the chandelier we had hanging from the ceiling.

I looked down. There, in the dim light below me, was the bed. There were two figures lying in the bed. To the right was my wife. Beside her was someone else. Both seemed asleep. This was a strange dream, I thought. I was curious. Whom would I dream to be in bed with my wife? I looked more closely, and the shock was intense. I was the someone on the bed!

My reaction was almost instantaneous. Here I was, there was my body. I was dying, this was death, and I wasn't ready to die. Somehow, the vibrations were killing me. Desperately, like a diver, I swooped down to my body and dove in. I then felt the bed and the covers, and when I opened my eyes, I was looking at the room from the perspective of my bed.

What had happened? Had I truly almost died? My heart was beating rapidly, but not unusually so. I moved my arms and legs. Everything seemed normal. The vibrations had faded away.[1]

Monroe is the best-known modern spokesperson for, and describer of, astral projection. His 1971 book, *Journeys out of the Body*, sparked a renaissance in the popularity of this transformative practice. When the unfamiliar experiences first blindsided him in 1958, for all he knew he was the only person ever thus gifted—or afflicted. And yet, the subject enjoys a rich and storied history stretching back millennia. Diverse spiritual traditions have enshrined out-of-body travel as a means to enlightenment, including, but not limited to, ancient Egyptian, Judaic and Christian, Hindu, Taoist, Japanese, Chinese, South American Amazonian, Inuit, and Western esotericism. For instance, in the sixth-century Hindu scriptures Yoga Vasishta-Maharamayana, the following guidance can be found, as related by Indian spiritual teacher Meher Baba in his *Discourses* (1967).

> In the advancing stages leading to the beginning of the path, the aspirant becomes spiritually prepared for the free use of the astral body. He may then undertake astral journeys, leaving the physical body in sleep or wakefulness. The astral journeys that are taken unconsciously are much less important than those undertaken with full consciousness and as a result of deliberate volition. This implies conscious use of the astral body. Conscious separation of the astral body from the outer vehicle of the gross body has its own value in making the soul feel its distinction from the gross body. One can, at will, put on and take off the external gross body as if it were a cloak, and use the astral body in undertaking journeys through it, if and when necessary.... The ability to undertake astral journeys therefore involves considerable expansion of one's scope for experience. It brings opportunities for promoting one's own spiritual advancement.[2]

Gradations of density

Fourteen hundred years later, Monroe was becoming more familiar with the process of leaving and returning to his body, refining his level of control. As I would frame it, he found that he could modulate the

IM/OM ratio through conscious intent, such that his OM envirohment became *partially* permeable. Countless others report this same hybrid density during the beginning phase of their practice.

> I was lying in bed just before sleep. The vibrations came and I wearily and patiently waited for them to pass so I could go to sleep. My arm was draped over the bed, fingers just brushing the rug. Idly, I tried to move my fingers and found I could scratch the rug. I pushed with the tips of my fingers against the rug. After a moment's resistance, they seemed to penetrate the rug and touch the floor underneath. With mild curiosity, I pushed my hand down farther. My fingers went through the floor and there was the rough upper surface of the ceiling of the room below. I felt around, and there was a small triangular piece of wood, a bent nail, and some sawdust.[3]

Later, as his density decreased, his mobility increased.

> I lay down in the bedroom about three in the afternoon, went into a relaxation pattern, felt the warmth (high-order vibrations), then thought heavily of the desire to "go" to R.W.
>
> There was the familiar sensation of movement through a light blue blurred area, then I was in what seemed to be a kitchen. R.W. was seated in a chair to the right. She had a glass in her hand. She was looking to my left, where two girls (about seventeen or eighteen, one blond and one brunette) also were sitting, each with glasses in their hands drinking something. The three of them were in conversation, but I could not hear what they were saying.
>
> I first approached the two girls, directly in front of them, but I could not attract their attention. I then turned to R.W., and I asked if she knew I was there.
>
> "Oh yes, I know you are here," she replied (mentally, as she was still in conversation with the two girls).
>
> I asked if she was sure that she would remember that I had been there. "Oh, I will definitely remember," the reply came.

I said that I was going to make sure that she remembered.

"I will remember, I'm sure I will," R.W. said, still in oral conversation with the girls.

I stated that I had to be sure she would remember, so I was going to pinch her.

"Oh, you don't need to do that, I'll remember," R.W. said hastily.

I said I had to be sure, so I reached over and tried to pinch her, gently, 1 thought. I pinched her in the side, just above the hips and below the ribcage. She let out a good loud "Ow!" and I backed up, because I was somewhat surprised. I really hadn't expected to be able actually to pinch her.

Satisfied that I had made some impression, at the least, I turned and left, thought of the physical, and was back almost immediately. I got up and went over to the typewriter where I am now. R.W. will not be back until Monday, and then I can determine if I made the contact, or if it was another unidentifiable miss. Time of return, three thirty-five.

Important aftermath: It is Tuesday after the Saturday. Here is what she reported today: On Saturday between three and four was the only time there was not a crowd of people in the beach cottage where she was staying. For the first time, she was alone with her niece (dark-haired, about eighteen) and the niece's friend (about the same age, blond). They were in the kitchen-dining area of the cottage from about three-fifteen to four, and she was having a drink, and the girls were having Cokes. They were doing nothing but sitting and talking.

I asked R.W. if she remembered anything else, and she said no. I questioned her more closely, but she could not remember anything more. Finally, in impatience, I asked her if she remembered the pinch. A look of complete astonishment crossed her face.

"Was that you?" She stared at me for a moment, then went into the privacy of my office, turned, and lifted

(just slightly) the edge of her sweater where it joined
her skirt on her left side. There were two brown and
blue marks at exactly the spot where I had pinched her.
"I was sitting there, talking to the girls," R.W. said,
"when all of a sudden I felt this terrible pinch. I must
have jumped a foot. I thought my brother-in-law had
come back and sneaked up behind me. I turned around,
but there was no one there. I never had any idea it was
you! It hurt!"

I apologized for pinching so hard, and she obtained
from me a promise that if I tried any such thing again, I
would do something other than a pinch that hard.[4]

The silver cord

Writer Alfred Ballabene reports that during his own out-of-body experiences, "glue-like strings" appear as the astral body tries to separate itself from the physical body. As the two move further apart, some of the strings break and clump into a specific and smaller region—typically the head, breast, back, stomach, or abdomen.

This strange umbilicus seems to be a literal manifestation of the interplay between the consciousness field and the other fundamental fields. The image has a deep history; Ecclesiastes 12:6-7 reads,

> Before ever the silver cord be loosed...
> Then shall the dust return to the Earth as it was:
> and the spirit shall return unto God.

This is the only such reference in the Bible. Some interpret it to refer simply to the spinal cord, but the Hebrew word for "loosed" suggests being removed far away, and since it's difficult to understand how or why the spine would typically be removed at death, it seems best to take the whole phrase as referring to the severing of body and spirit.

On January 9, 1961, Robert Monroe experimentally tested this concept.

> I decided to see if there truly was a "cord" between the
> physical and the Second Body. In the past, I had not
> noticed any, except for an odd tugging action at times.
> I worked out of the body via axis rotation and
> remained in the room several feet up and away from
> the physical body. I turned to look for the "cord," but it

was not visible. Then I reached to see if I could feel it coming out the front, top, or back of my head. As I reached the back of my head, my hand brushed against something, and I felt behind me with both hands. Whatever it was extended out from a spot in my back directly between my shoulder blades, not from the head, as I'd expected. I felt the base, and it was exactly like the spread-out roots of a tree radiating from the trunk. The roots slanted outward and into my back down as far as the middle of my torso, up to my neck, and into the shoulders on each side. I reached outward, and it formed into a two-inch-thick cable. It was hanging loosely, and I could feel its texture very definitely. It was body-warm to the touch and seemed to be composed of hundreds of tendonlike strands packed neatly together, but not twisted or spiraled. It was flexible and seemed to have no skin covering.[5]

In a 2010 blog post, afterlife researcher Michael Tymn reports that end-of-life caregivers in South Africa, along with psychiatrist B. J. Laubscher, have observed at patients' deaths

a ribbon-like cord stretching from the back of the spirit's head to the body below. The spirit would begin to glow as it fully formed. As it righted itself, the connecting cord thinned out as if it was fraying away. As Laubscher came to understand it, the material...acts as a sort of "glue" in bonding the physical body with the spirit body, and the more materialistic a person, the denser the [glue] and the more difficulty the person has in "giving up the ghost."[6]

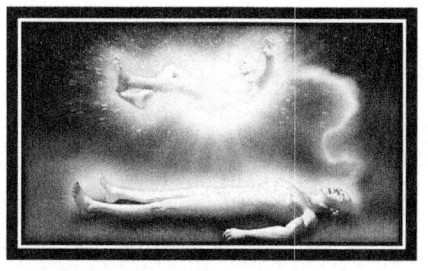

At the age of six, medium Eileen Garrett, whom we met in section 5.1, unfortunately strangled several ducks at the edge of a pond.

I looked at the ducks lying limp on the grass beside me and almost hoped they might still be alive. But at this moment something really startling did begin to happen. The ducks were quiet but there was a movement going on all around them. I saw, curling up from each little body a grey smoke-like substance, rising in spiral form. This fluid stuff began to move and curl as it rose, and gradually I saw it take on new shape as it moved away from the bodies of these little dead ducks.

Fear had now given way to amazement in the face of this spectacle. I was joyful because I knew in that moment that the ducks were "coming alive" again. I had forgotten about their dead bodies lying limp below and waited, with tense expectancy, to see them take on new shape.

I began to wonder whether all other creatures also had this same fashion of escaping from life, as did these ducks. The only way to find out for certain was to begin to kill something else and watch what followed. The only important thing for me now was to discover whether or not death brought forth new life; and if this were true, what kind of life did death produce?

For two weeks crows and little rabbits became the victims of my search for knowledge. Then, of a sudden, came a terrible revulsion against myself for all this killing that I had done. The startling truth now came to me in a flash. I had seen enough to know by then that I had killed nothing at all, but only had changed its form.[7]

Our own replicas

Louisa May Alcott wrote of attending a deathbed vigil and watching "a light mist rise from the body, float up, and vanish in the air." Her mother saw it too. In *The Art of Dying*, Peter and Elizabeth Fenwick chronicle many such experiences. In the case of a woman attending the death of her sister: "I saw a fast-moving will-o'-the-wisp appear to leave her body by the side of her mouth. The shock and the beauty of it made me gasp. It appeared like a fluid or gaseous diamond, pristine, sparkly, and pure. It moved rapidly upwards and was gone."[75]

Raymond Moody also discusses this phenomenon in his book *Glimpses of Eternity*. "Some say it looks like smoke, while others say it is as subtle as steam. Sometimes, it seems to have a human shape. It usually drifts upwards and disappears fairly quickly."[8]

In another 2010 blog post, Michael Tymn writes that

> Moody and [*Glimpses of Eternity*] co-author Paul Perry quote a Georgia doctor who twice saw a mist coming up from deceased patients. The doctor explained that as the patients died they lit up with a bright glow, their eyes shining with a silvery light. The mist formed over the chest and hovered there, as the doctor observed closely and saw that the mist had depth and complex structure. He further said that it seemed to have layers with energetic motion in it. A hospice psychologist is quoted as saying that the misty clouds which form above the head or chest seem to have an electrical component to them. A nurse reported seeing a mist rising from many patients as they die, including her father, with whom she saw the mist rise from his chest "as if off a still river," and then hover for a few seconds before dissipating.
>
> The bright glow witnessed by the Georgia doctor has also been reported by many other deathbed witnesses. Moody quotes one man as finding that the room became "uncomfortably bright," so bright that he couldn't shut it out even when he closed his eyes. A hospice nurse reported seeing a "luminous presence floating near the bed, shaped somewhat like a person."
>
> Moody tells of his own experience as he and other family members gathered at the bed of his dying mother. Among some other strange things, they all saw an unusual glow in the room. "It was like looking at light in a swimming pool at night," Moody explains.
>
> There are countless reports of dying people themselves having visions of light and seeing loved ones gathering, but skeptics discount them as hallucinations.

However, as Moody points out, it is one thing to claim that the dying person is hallucinating, but quite another to claim that healthy people in the room are sharing in the hallucination.

A vapor lay "parallel with the dying person and about two feet above the body," B.J.F Laubscher wrote in *Beyond Life's Curtain*. "Gradually, this cloudlike appearance became denser and took on the form, first vaguely and then more definitely, of the person in the bed. This process continued until the phantom suspended above the body was an absolute replica of the person, especially the face."

In *Out-of-the-Body Experiences*, Dr. Robert Crookall quotes Dr. R. B. Hout, a physician who was present at the death of his aunt. "My attention was called…to something immediately above the physical body, suspended in the atmosphere about two feet above the bed. At first, I could distinguish nothing more than the vague outline of a hazy, fog-like substance. There seemed to be only a mist held suspended, motionless. But, as I looked, very gradually there grew into my sight a denser, more solid condensation of this vapor. Then I was astonished to see definite outlines presenting themselves, and soon I saw this substance was assuming a human form." Hout then saw that the form resembled the physical body of his aunt. It hung suspended horizontally a few feet above the body. When the phantom form appeared complete, Hout saw his aunt's features clearly.[9]

There is even a well-known syndrome in which the subtle body/consciousness stages an "impossible" resurgence moments *before* death. In cases of "terminal lucidity," a person who has been mentally absent for years, whose brain has been essentially destroyed by Alzheimer's disease, Lewy body dementia, cancer, etc., suddenly returns to their old self, memory, cognition, personality fully restored in order to reconnect with loved ones at their bedside. As the brain is dying, the mind is freed. Researcher Stafford Betty likens such events to the sun's glorious re-emergence after a total eclipse; for more the brain as inhibitor of mind, see Appendix K.

The Kluski hand casts

Even after transitioning, our finespun new selves can occasionally reverse course, lowering our vibration again for a brief return. It's difficult; one spirit reported, "It's like climbing out of a swimming pool with a heavy overcoat on."[10] And though we ourselves still feel solid and whole—our physical design is as *normal* now as before—those on Earth typically fail to perceive us. Unless, for instance, our visit is hosted by an established physical medium.

Franek Kluski (1873-1943) was one such medium, extensively investigated by Nobel Prize-winning physiologist Charles Richet. In 1921, Richet conducted an experiment that succeeded in producing the most important and enduring "primal artifacts" in the long history of psychic/spiritual research.

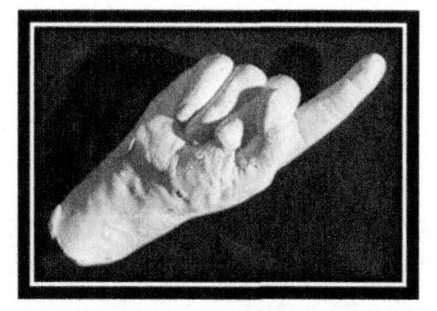

During these trials, Kluski's séances were, as usual, graced by spirit forms. For the first time, though, they were asked to submerge one hand or both into a bowl of molten paraffin wax that had been placed on the table—the sitters could hear quiet splashing in the dark—and then to remove the wax-coated hand(s) from the bowl, wait for the wax to quickly dry, and then to dematerialize, leaving the remaining "wax glove" on the table. As the wax was thin and delicate, any ordinary hand would be unable to withdraw itself without causing breakage. As Richet explains in his classic *Thirty Years of Psychical Research* (1923),

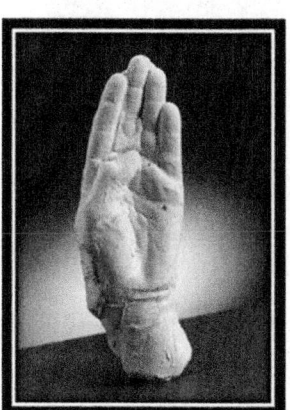

> By reason of the narrowness at the wrist, these molds could not be obtained by living hands, for the whole hand would have to be withdrawn through the narrow opening at the wrist.... Dematerialization...was necessary to disengage the hand from the paraffin "glove."[11]

Later, plaster of Paris was gingerly poured into the hardened molds, resulting in remarkable casts that are still preserved at The Institut Métapsychique International in Paris. Almost none of them are full-sized, though in all other respects they match adult hands in shape and line markings. They range from small child through to small adult size.

With his collaborator, physician Gustav Geley, Richet devised a clever safeguard.

> Geley and I took the precaution of introducing, unknown to any other person, a small quantity of cholesterin in the bath of melted paraffin wax placed before the medium during the séance. This substance is soluble in paraffin, but on adding sulfuric acid it takes on a deep violet-red tint, so that we could be absolutely certain that any molds obtained should be from the paraffin provided by ourselves and could not have been prepared in advance.[12]

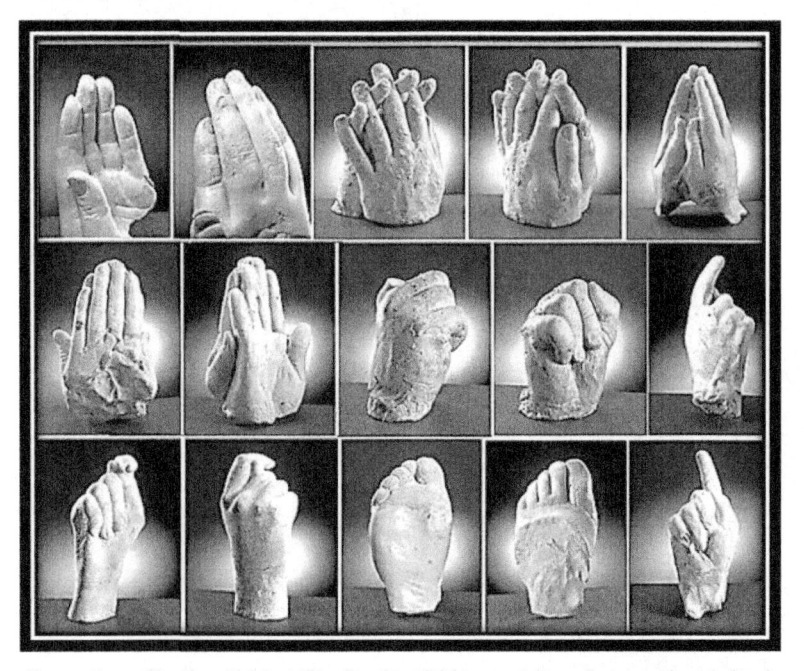

From the collection held at The Institut Métapsychique International, Paris.

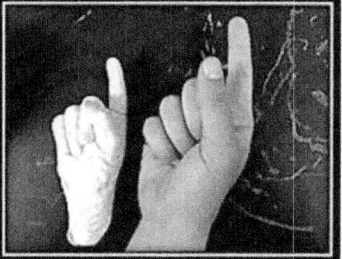

Leslie Kean visiting the collection, 2017; the hands are smaller than hers.

References

1. Robert Monroe, *Journeys Out of the Body*, Doubleday, New York: 1971.
2. Meher Baba, *Discourses by Meher Baba* (Vol. 1), Adi K. Irani, Ahmednagar, India: 1967.
3. Monroe, op. cit.
4. Ibid.
5. Ibid.
6. Michael Tymn's blog, WhiteCrowBooks.com
7. Eileen Garrett, *My Life as a Search for the Meaning of Mediumship*, Oquaga Press, New York: 1939.
8. Raymond Moody, *Glimpses of Eternity*, Guideposts Books, New York: 2010.
9. Tymn, op. cit.
10. Leslie Kean, *Surviving Death: A Journalist Investigates Evidence for an Afterlife*, Crown Archetype, New York: 2017.
11. Charles Richet, *Thirty Years of Psychical Research*, Macmillan, New York: 1923.
12. Ibid.

Appendix E
Gaining Substance: Franek Kluski's Séances

The same physical medium, Franek Kluski, who set the stage for the famous hand molds presented at the end of Appendix D, can also help us understand how low-density spirits can, under the right circumstances, take on greater heft and definition. They borrow OM from their immediate surroundings, and then mold it to their ends. In *Other Realities? The Enigma of Franek Kluski's Mediumship*, biographer Zofia Weaver describes this process.

> If a séance took place in a room with lots of furniture and ornaments, and the participants' clothing was varied, the phantoms seemed to have no problem dressing themselves. They were felt to rub various objects prior to appearing, as if transforming the "raw material" into what was needed. When officers in Russian uniforms appeared, the officers present at the séance felt their epaulettes and buttons being rubbed, after which the phantoms' epaulettes and buttons would shine.
>
> Phantoms also seemed to rub against the soft furnishings, and the clothing of all those present, particularly Kluski, showed signs of wear after a séance. Okołowicz found that his own clothing looked as if someone had brushed it with a very sharp brush and given it a violent beating. The fabric would become worn and threadbare. At one sitting (on 26 January 1925), the medium wore dark-red silk pajamas, which he had only worn two or three times previously, and wore for the first time at a séance. After the séance, the garment was found to be totally worn through in places, like a web.
>
> Another example comes from the séance on 10 June 1924, when a participant felt her string of pearls being rubbed and then an exotic female phantom appeared (self-illuminating)

with a large string of pearls. When compared, the phantom's string of pearls turned out to be longer and the pearls larger. This "doubling" or "duplicating" was quite frequent, and most often involved Kluski's clothing.

Besides receiving such material assistance, the spirits also often benefited from collective emotional or spiritual focus. This makes sense, of course, given that both visiting spirits and séance sitters inhabit one and the same fundamental consciousness field; the greater the mutual resonance, the stronger the effect.

> It was very often observed that, for example, an officer's phantom would have a clearly detailed military cap, but the uniform would be a blur, vaguely resembling what the medium was wearing at the time. However, when attention was paid to the uniform, the phantom seemed to "grow" one. Or a phantom would appear, not very clearly but, on approaching a person who recognised it with emotion, it would gradually become clearer both to that person and to others close by. On the other hand, on moving further away, it would lose some of its expressiveness and individuality for the other participants, as if the emotional "support" was involved in its creation.

> Sometimes, they [the materializing spirits] were partial or undersized: "Two thirds, even one-half of the natural size. When I first saw such an apparition," wrote Kluski's close friend Norbert Okołowicz, "I thought it was that of a child, but a closer examination revealed the wrinkled face of an old man or woman. The leader of the séance would say then, 'Let us help the medium' and would begin to beat time, so that the sitters might breathe simultaneously and deeply. The effect of this procedure is wonderful: The undersized apparition grows and in several seconds reaches full size."

> [By the same token,] it seemed to the participants—350 over several years—that the more alive the apparitions seemed, the more like a husk became the appearance of the medium. Okołowicz describes a situation after one of the séances when he returned to the study and found Kluski lying motionless on the settee. He realised that the medium had not woken up from his trance, which manifested itself by the total rigidity of the body and spasmodically curled fingers. Okołowicz decided to place him in a more comfortable position and

noticed with surprise that he was extremely light. Okołowicz put his hand under Kluski's hips and tried to lift him. This was easily achieved. When finally, after a lot of effort, managed to unclench the man's fist, the whole body regained its normal state of flexibility, and when he immediately afterwards tried to lift Kluski he found that his weight was back to normal.[1]

See sections 4.3 and 4.4 for my discussion of the process of ratio exchange between IM and OM.

References

1. Zofia Weaver, *Other Realities? The Enigma of Franek Kluski's Mediumship*, White Crow Books, Guildford, UK: 2015.

Appendix F
Signatures of Macro-PK

Physicist Kevin Knuth has offered some helpful analysis with regard to UAPs and energy. In "APEC 8/28, Part #2 - Kevin Knuth - Flight Characteristics & Physics of UAP" on the Alt Propulsion channel, Knuth cites the well-known Tic Tac case, in which radar aboard the USS Nimitz tracked the craft descending from 28,000 feet to sea level in less than a second. The estimated velocity involved here is Mach 60, or about 46,000 mph—which translates to a g-force of 5000.

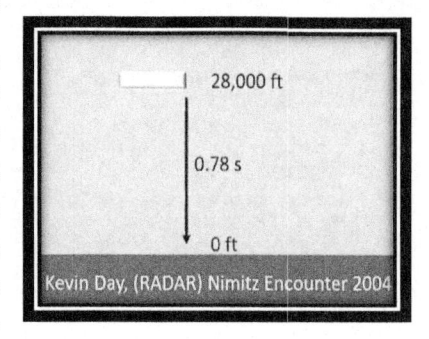

Nor is this rate an outlier; numerous comparable UAP velocities were registered on radar as far back as the 1950s.[1]

A striking feature of such maneuvers is that they produce *no detectable energy signatures*. "That's a crazy amount of kinetic energy," Knuth points out, "and it shouldn't just disappear when the object stops. At minimum, in the case of the Tic Tac, it should have deposited the equivalent of 100 tons of TNT, but none of that is observed."[2]

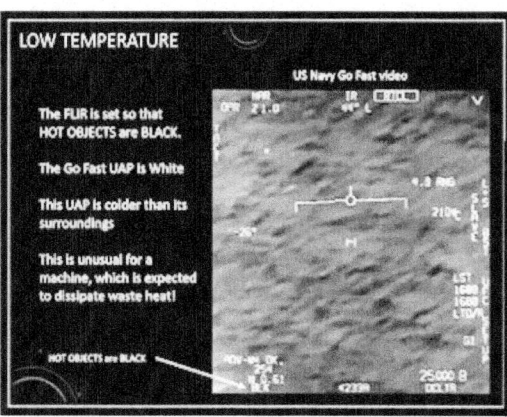

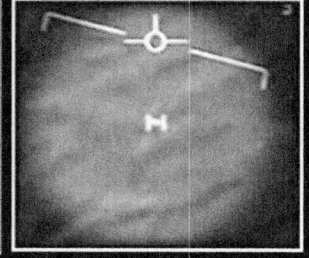

Quite the contrary, as we saw in section 5.4, thermal readings reveal that these craft are typically cold, which not only directly contradicts the first law of thermodynamics (the conservation of energy) but also runs counter to the popular "warp drive" hypothesis of UAP propulsion. Under this hypothesis, what registers as uniformly cold should instead a dual signature—hotter at the trailing edge of the craft.

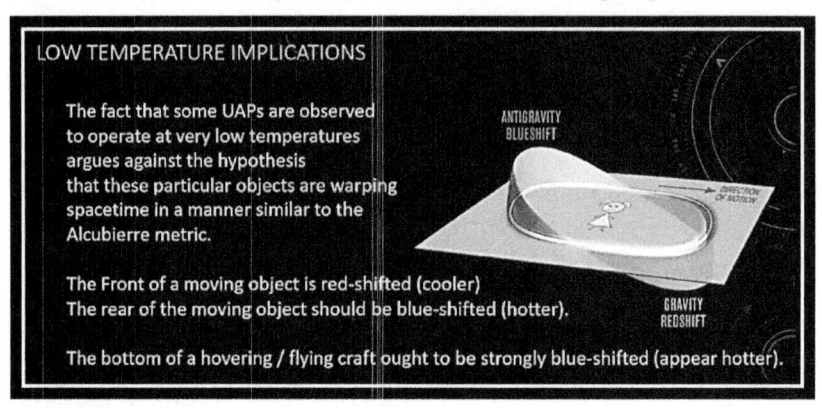

> **LOW TEMPERATURE IMPLICATIONS**
>
> The fact that some UAPs are observed to operate at very low temperatures argues against the hypothesis that these particular objects are warping spacetime in a manner similar to the Alcubierre metric.
>
> ANTIGRAVITY BLUESHIFT
>
> DIRECTION OF MOTION
>
> The Front of a moving object is red-shifted (cooler)
> The rear of the moving object should be blue-shifted (hotter).
>
> GRAVITY REDSHIFT
>
> The bottom of a hovering / flying craft ought to be strongly blue-shifted (appear hotter).

Thermal cameras can sometimes reach across the visibility threshold. Knuth and colleagues have analyzed footage of objects that do not appear in the visible spectrum but do show up (cold) on thermal cameras.[3]

According to the MTR theory, all matter in our earthly world is *hybrid* matter, and it's the IM/OM ratio that determines how reality manifests. If UAPs appear and disappear by means of ratio modulation, and if they can come into view—like apparitions—even while possessing much, *much* lower density than ordinary objects, and thus proportionally lower kinetic energy, then what has been so deeply puzzling when seen through the lens of conventional physics becomes legible. The energy-dissipation problem *itself* dissipates to zero once we're dealing with a different class of object altogether, lacking thrust. The "five observables" seem to be violations of physics only when seen within the constraints of small-m materialism, not under the broad, forgiving regime of Materialism.

When UAPs descend low or touch down, they are at their densest and then do engage with the electromagnetic spectrum; witnesses get burned; electronics die; sparks fly; etc. When they're on the go, they default—as it were—to fairy dust.

Another mystifying episode in our recent past may—just *may*—be susceptible to a UAP-related interpretation as a dramatic instance of macro-K. The infamous 2014 disappearance of the Malaysian airliner, MH370, has attracted renewed attention with the release of satellite and drone footage of the plane being surrounded and dogged by three swiftly circling orbs. At a certain point, it simply vanishes amid what appears at first to be an explosion. It's not an explosion in any conventional sense, however, because its thermal signature reads *cold*. I'd suggest that perhaps the entire plane is being apported; see sections and 4.8. Its IM/OM ratio is spiked, chilling the jet and forcing it across the visibility threshold. Whether MH370 was teleported elsewhere remains an open question. See Ashton Forbes' in-depth analysis, "The Untold Story of Malaysian Flight MH370" on The Confessionals channel.

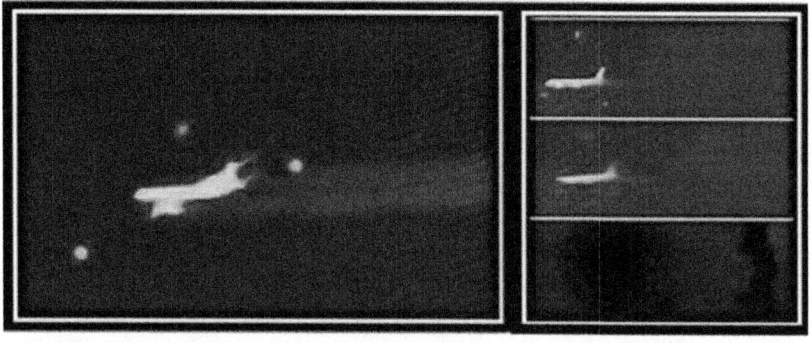

The plane and pursuing objects are hot (bright).   **The plane vanishes; black = cold**

References

1. Knuth, Powell, and Reali, "Estimating Flight Characteristics of Anomalous Unidentified Aerial Vehicles," *Entropy* 2019, 21(10), 939.
2. Ibid.
3. Ibid

Appendix G

Dusty Old Books Ahead of their Time:
Invisible Matter Precursors

> The more inexplicable a phenomenon appears, the deeper is it rooted, the greater is the significance it bears, the bigger is the interest adhering to it, and the more pressing is the challenge for science to examine and to explain it.
> —Karl von Reichenbach

> The Psychic is a person in whom there is an abnormal capacity for dislocation in the normal relationship of Soul and body.
> —Edward W. Cox

The ancient concept of *aether*—an all-pervasive substance that acts as a medium for all otherwise unexplainable phenomena—was reintroduced in several forms across the centuries.

The Psychic Force

In section 4.5, we covered Barrie G. Colvin's acoustic analysis showing that psychic/spiritual knocks, or "raps," are made not *on* walls and tables but *within* walls and tables. I have since learned that the same recognition was shared nearly 140 years earlier by Edward W. Cox (1809-1879) in *Spiritualism Answered by Science*, though he rejects any supernatural interpretation. "The Psychic Force," as he calls it,

> operates…altogether unlike muscular force. It is neither a blow, a push, nor a pressure. If the subject of the experiment be a table, for instance, the sounds are not upon the surface, as if something had struck the wood, but as if they were produced in the fibrous centre of the slab.[1]

Cox even reports the use of a simple medical instrument to confirm this interiority and the onset of the phenomenon during séances.

> First come delicate sounds, audible only by help of a stethoscope; then these grow louder, and can be heard by the ear and felt by the hand; and then come the motions [such as table tilting and full levitation] that noperson who has once witnessed them can either imagine or mistake.[2]

And he goes further, offering a tentative conjecture that approaches Dean Radin's much later insight that macro-PK does not involve "imposing anything from the outside, it's doing something that happens way down deep at the microscopic scale and changes the information structure from the inside." Cox concedes that his terminology is imprecise. "We call it a 'force' for convenience," he writes,

> and for lack of a better term; but it is…more in the nature of an influence than of motion of particles projected and impinging on other bodies and by the impact causing motions and sounds on the bodies struck.[3]

Leslie Kean's description of levitation in section 3.7—"The table…swayed and dipped, gliding as if riding on waves. 'It was spongy, like pushing down on a spring.'"—chimes with Cox's attempt to understand his conjectured "influence."

> [It] appears to diffuse itself over the entire body to which it is applied, and to exercise itself in any part of that body with equal power and facility…. [It is] in the nature of diffusion and inflation, seeming to diffuse itself through the whole substance of the thing moved.

His construal of the phenomenon also dovetails with my own sense that simple buoyancy is responsible (see section 4.3).

> Thus, if it be a table, it is raised, not as by a force applied below, but as if by the levitation of the material of which it is composed. When it rises from the floor it mounts like a balloon. If the hand is pressed upon it in its ascent, the sensation is that of a floating body rising because it is lighter than the air.[4]

Scientists, even parapsychologists, don't seem to talk like this anymore, in plain language with concrete, easy-to-picture analogies—like I'm talking about my MTR theory—but I find that psychic/spiritual phenomena occurring still today can marry well with certain antiquarian sources, provided no better ideas have cropped up in between.

Magnetic fluid

Cox was working in the prominent tradition of Franz Mesmer (1734-1815), who famously proposed an natural influence that he called *magnetic fluid* or *animal magnetism*, which became for a time the leading explanation for what we call macro-PK effects. This was back when the unseen push and pull of magnets was still beyond comprehension, before Maxwell and Hertz discovered the electromagnetic field. How, Mesmer asked,

> can a body act upon another at a distance, without there being something to establish a communication between them? We suppose that a substance emanates from him who magnetizes [what we today would call a hypnotist] and is conveyed to the person magnetized, in the direction given it by the will. This substance...we call the *magnetic fluid*, a subtle and mobile fluid, which pervades the universe and associates all things together in mutual intercourse and harmony.[5]

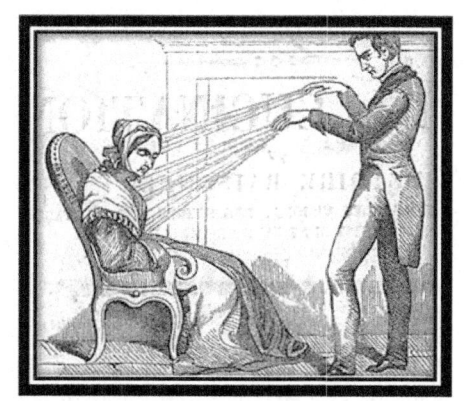

This sounds like a dead ringer, doesn't it, for what's described by quantum field theory (section 2.3)? During Mesmer's time, though, the existence of this fluid, much less its cosmic reach, was just an imaginative shot in the dark, a lucky guess.

> The nature of this fluid is unknown; even its existence has not been demonstrated; but everything occurs as if it did exist. [6]

In 2024, our collective search for the medium of psychic/spiritual magic never seems to lean upon Mesmer's cosmology. We're at least a couple of steps ahead of the eighteenth century; the existence of universal "fluids" *has* now been demonstrated by quantum physics, and we've also succeeded in recognizing IM—my nomination for Mesmer's "subtle and mobile fluid"—by its most generalized gravitational effect upon OM fields (section 4.1), though without yet gaining the finer focus that will be needed to reveal its concrete role in the target phenomena.

Odic fluid

Another concept currently cast aside as quaintly obsolete—but that I call a promising forerunner—is that of *Od*, or *odic fluid*, a typically invisible substance associated with all matter and permeating the entire universe. Karl von Reichenbach (1788-1869) coined the term in homage to the Norse god Odin.

> Od describes a kind of pervasive universal life- or energy-force detectable by a select few "sensitives." Odic energy was said to surround us everywhere. It seemed related to electricity, magnets, crystals, heat, light, and chemical actions, according to various sources. And some people could consciously manifest it.[7]

Von Reichenbach sought to prove the existence of odic fluid through a variety of experiments, just two of which I'll touch on here. First, he chronicled[8] the acute visual abilities of certain rare people who were able, in a pitch-dark room, to see light emanating from plants,

> notably from their flowers. Some of the higher sensitives stated that the flowers illuminated the whole room so that they were able to distinguish objects in it, and some even described minute details of blossoms and were even able to determine plant species. These odic emanations were only visible with fresh or living plants, withering plants lost their shine.[9]

If all living beings possess consciousness, broadly speaking, it makes sense that it would be discernable, in principle, by other conscious agents. By whatever name, this medium shares the matter/energy duality with all other fundamental fields, and as energy it can manifest as illumination like glowing orbs, radiant spirits, and auras around organisms.

Second, von Reichenbach ran numerous trials with psychically gifted subjects able to produce macro-PK, the muscle-independent movement of objects. For instance, he documented table tipping—like that achieved by Ariel Farias (section 3.7)—and concluded that, in this context, the odic fluid was "capable of being either directly accumulated on, or transferred by distribution to, other bodies [objects]."[10] Although it stops just shy of recognizing matter-type ratio as such, this description sounds akin to my proposed explanation for macro-PK as a build-up of IM within an object, reducing its density and rendering it lighter than air.

Conscious intent

In order to accomplish macro-PK, the fundamental consciousness field has to be a fellow form of matter/energy, but it must also be made of a different kind of information, one that is, unlike the others, animated by thought.

Agénor de Gasparin (1810-1871) conducted hundreds of table tipping experiments and was among the first to systematically demonstrate the strict "obedience" of the phenomenon to the volition of the subject(s), once the close connection was established. Besides recognizing that the invisible fluid involved must be a physical—not strictly a supernatural—substance, de Gasparin wrote that "the fluid is directed by the will sometimes to one leg of the table and sometimes to another. The table becomes in some sense part of ourselves, becomes [by extension] one of our limbs and carries out the movement we think of in the same way as does our arm."[11] Likewise, Farias says he feels as if he is "merging" with the wood during levitation trials.

Density

Johannes Greber (1874-1944), a German Catholic priest, picked up on Reichenbach's theory in his *Communication with the Spirit World, Its*

Laws and Purpose, which records hundreds of hours' worth of messages received through trance mediumship and automatic writing. He was told by purported spirits about a substance so fine and subtle that it can be perceived only under rare circumstances.

> As you [on Earth] are able to convert water into steam, and even to cause steam to become invisible to the human eye, so also is the spirit world able to dissolve matter completely.[12]

This seems to allude to the process behind apportation, spirit materializations/dematerializations, as well as to the fluctuating solidity of UAPs and their occupants. Greber's informants adopted Reichenbach's term in completing the account.

> Matter which has been converted into Od can be transported to any place whatever, there to be condensed anew into matter.[13]

He testifies that he learned Od's even deeper secret, which we too marveled at in section 3.5—that no information is ever lost or inaccessible.

> Od reflects your entire existence; every act, every utterance, every thought of yours is reproduced by it as in a film. It is a "Book of Life," into which everything is entered.[14]

Cold

All of these early researchers noted the same "psychic breeze" and sharp lowering of temperature in association with psychic events, the effect that I ascribed, in section 4.6, to a sudden rise in the IM/OM ratio. In *Parapsychology*, after surveying the various historical notions of a universal fluid, René Sudre (1880-1968) writes that, "Observing its coincidence with the breeze, that is to say with the emission of fluid, we cannot help comparing this phenomenon with the expansion of gas under reduced pressure."[15] This insight runs parallel to my proposition that a burgeoning of IM within a room, say, will thin the atmosphere, lowering the kinetic energy (heat) and creating a pressure differential (breeze); I'm happy to discover this suggested already, so long ago.

References

1. Edward W. Cox, *Spiritualism Answered by Science*, Longman & Co., London: 1871.
2. Ibid.
3. Ibid.
4. Ibid.
5. Deleuze, J.P.F.,*Practical Instruction in Animal Magnetism*, Hippolyte Baillière, London: 1852.
6. Ibid.
7. Jim Dee, "Od: A Mysterious, Hypothetical Life- or Energy-Force Proposed by Baron Carl von Reichenbach," Medium.com
8. Karl von Reichenbach. *Die Pflanzenwelt in Ihren Beziehungen Zur Sensitivität Und Zum Ode*, Wilhelm Braumüller Publishers, Osterreich, Germany: 1858.
9. Michael Nahn, "The Sorcerer of Cobenzl and His Legacy: The Life of Baron Karl Ludwig von Reichenbach, His Work and Its Aftermath," *Journal of Scientific Exploration*, Vol. 26, No. 2, 2012.
10. Karl von Reichenbach, *Researches on Magnetism, Electricity, Heat, Light, Crystallization and Chemical Attraction in Relation to the Vital Force*, Taylor, Walton and Maberly, London: 1849.
11. Agénor de Gasparin, *Les tables tournantes du surnaturel en general et des esprits, par le Cte*, Bonaventure and Ducessois for E. Dentu, Paris: 1854.
12. Johannes Greber, *Communication with the Spirit World: Its Laws and Purpose*, John Felsberg, Inc., New York: 1932.
13. Ibid.
14. Ibid.
15. René Sudre, *Parapsychology*, Citadel Press, New York: 1960.

Appendix H
Dr. Paul Werbos and the "Symbiotic Noosphere"

After learning of historical research that seems to prefigure my MTR theory (Appendix G), I was pleased as well to find a leading contemporary thinker, Paul J. Werbos, who sees dark matter as the seat of consciousness.

Born in 1947, Werbos is a mathematician and engineer known for his groundbreaking contributions to the fields of neural networks, machine learning, and artificial intelligence. His Harvard Ph.D. is in applied mathematics. He was one of the original three two-year Presidents of the International Neural Network Society (INNS), and for twenty-five years served as a program director at the National Science Foundation.

In *Cosmos and History: The Journal of Natural and Social Philosophy,* Werbos writes of the *noosphere*, a term coined by Philippe Teilhard de Chardin (1881-1955) to supplement *biosphere*, *atmosphere*, etc. *Noos* is Greek for "mind," and the noosphere is a realm of consciousness no less physically real than other natural earthly spheres. Its reach, however, is immeasurably greater.

In seeking "a possible scientific basis for the flow of energy (often called *qi*) central to all authentic spiritual traditions around the world," Werbos identifies an obvious candidate.

> In order to be consistent with the best mainstream version of quantum theory known to science today...while still accepting spiritual energy or psi [psychic phenomena], we have almost no choice but to hold that "dark matter" is the physical substrate which makes them possible. We may debate whether dark matter is made up of fields, or of particles, or of a mix of the two, but in any case, it is what Aristotle would call the "substance" underlying higher forms like spirit and...consciousness.[1]

While acknowledging that dark matter spreads throughout the universe in an unbroken "cosmic web," actively forming stars and galaxies, Werbos emphasizes its local role in the ubiquitous noosphere permeating our world and even animating us individually. A key aspect of his theory, he explains, "is that we humans are what Dante called 'half beast, half angel'—a symbiotic life form, such that part of us is the system of atoms that science now understands…and part is dark matter." Furthermore, "the dominant partner…is the dark matter side."[2]

Considering, for instance, such psi phenomena as macro-PK [e.g., object levitation], Werbos insists inarguably that "*Something* has to perturb ordinary matter for PK to be possible…and this has to be something we don't see with today's instruments."[3]

References

1. Paul J. Werbos, "The Phenomenon of Man, Revisited: Evolution and I.T. Versus Extinction in the Years to Come," *Cosmos and History: The Journal of Natural and Social Philosophy*, vol. 15, no. 1, 2019.
2. Ibid.
3. Ibid.

Appendix I

"But How Will I Survive as Vibration?"
Frequencies and their Informational Abundance

> *It isn't solid like on Earth, but it seems the same to us. If you came to my lovely garden, you wouldn't see anything. It would seem just air to you. Isn't that funny? If we didn't make our world out of thinking, there'd be nothing but light around us.*
> —Elizabeth, speaking through medium Geraldine Cummins

Someone asked me, "But how will I survive as vibration? That's way too insub*stantial*." I've been working on my answer.

We already do survive, moment by moment, in exactly this way. Einstein's famous "Everything is vibration" refers to the elementary particles whose very existence is defined by their respective frequencies. As living creatures, we feel so solid, but our bodies are made of atoms that are each 99.99999% empty space; if you were to suck all of it from the 8.2 billion human beings, our mass would fit comfortably into an average snow globe. If you enlarged the atoms of your hand until every nucleus was the size of an apple, there would be 1200 miles between every two "apples."

But that isn't even my answer. As we saw in sections 2.2 and 2.3, elementary particles themselves are not foundational; they're an effect of a deeper cause—fluidlike quantum fields. This means that living, breathing organisms like us do not ultimately depend for our existence upon any of the measurable properties, or even the ineffable qualities, of the atoms that make up the molecules that make up the cells that make up the tissues of our organs.

What is "substance" anyway?

That's not my answer either, because despite all of the above, the vibratory nature of all matter notwithstanding, it can still seem stubbornly impossible to conceive of being alive without this stable, meaty contraption we dress each morning.

What's needed is a whole separate paradigm, one that equates "life" not with breath, bone, and blood but with awareness, with information processing. Indeed, our core identity matches this paradigm already, though we don't commonly recognize it. Those undergoing near-death experiences and catching sight of their lifeless bodies from above find them instantly irrelevant—"I can't believe I thought I was *that* thing."

The driving question here, however, is not whether we transcend our bodies at death but exactly how to grasp the subsequent nature of a self. It's easy to *say*, as I confidently have throughout this book, that consciousness operates at a much higher frequency than earthly matter, or to quote authorities reporting that the environment of the afterlife is "so rarefied that it is invisible to the mortal eye and eludes the finest instruments of the scientists" (Frederic Myers). But who among us can understand this—I mean *truly* understand it—while still standing in the flesh on this planet?

Let's get better acquainted with the phenomenon of frequency, an aspect of nature that enjoys insufficient appreciation outside of elite specialist circles.

During the Internet Age, it's become hip to take every fresh technological advance in stride, but I confess I've never quite gotten over the radio. Flowing through every cubic inch in my house is the identical information, the clear Vermont Public Radio signal. I could carry my set outdoors and then tour a cubic mile, that's 254 trillion cubic inches, and each spot would mirror it, too—faithful replicas of sound. Some stations pervade tens of thousands of cubic miles, sharing them with countless other communication signals all vibrating at different rates.

In other words, "empty" space can be invisibly saturated with information, and frequency is the key. Granted, radio only primitively illustrates the point because of its meagre bandwidth, but as a proof of concept it allows us to extrapolate thanks to the distinction between kind and degree. Artificial Intelligence, soon to be ubiquitous in the air around us, beamed planet-wide by satellites, is based on the same *kind* of agency—computers still use radio waves—but its unfathomably greater *degree* of richness and flexibility, especially during the past five years of development, and its accelerating capacity to learn, already rival the wonders of thought itself. What more won't be achieved over the next century? ChatGBT 5 will seem like the steam engine seems to us today.

Of course, the debate over AI and human consciousness, their vaunted singularity, is likely eternal, but even in 2024 we can agree at least that it is a *serious* debate, and that it's already becoming harder and harder to identify dimensions of thinking that AI cannot emulate—and often exceed. This by itself is remarkable, a testament to the potential not just of information as technology but also of information as, yes, *selfhood*.

A self, a mind, is profoundly complex and subtle, but is it *infinitely* so?

Once frequencies are understood to carry information at all, the sky's the limit. Radio waves are the lowest-frequency type, the weakest and least data-rich on the spectrum. At the other end, gamma waves are *300 trillion times* more energetic than radio waves, able in theory to wield that much more information. We cannot use them to communicate, though, because this very extremity renders them unmanageable; they would pass right through any would-be receivers.

That's because our instruments, don't forget, are by definition composed of earthly materials. And yet, this is hardly a limiting factor on the informational potential of vibration as such. Recall, too, the exceedingly lower density of IM as contrasted with OM (sections 4.1 and 4.2), therefore the exceedingly higher frequencies—*even than gamma waves*—at which it operates, and here we have a framework within which we can begin to imagine the abundance available within the IM of the afterlife.

They have an energy all their own; as quoted in Appendix C,

> The spirits at Scole explained that they were not working with electricity as we know it but with an analogue form of energy that is common in their realm. "Don't fall into the misunderstanding that we are dealing with electromagnetic waves because we are not."

But no, not *only* "within the IM of the afterlife." IM *anywhere* has an energy all its own, on Earth as it is in Heaven. Pure IM without OM operates everywhere—*every cubic inch*—and its name is consciousness. It's the fundamental field that allows for telepathy and remote viewing (sections 3.2-3.4), for example, and its purity is the reason that, although both are obviously real, our parochial instruments have never captured even the slightest hint of their medium or mechanism.

The fact that every person on Earth can—or can be trained to—transcend bodily limits by sharing thoughts with far-off others or by remote viewing the contents of a book while blindfolded, a covert enemy submarine on the other side of the world, the rings of Jupiter, or a cousin's lost key, is thoroughly unsurprising. Consciousness is like that; it doesn't need to reach for information, only to attune to what it knows already (section 3.5). And what is attunement but resonance, finding the right frequency?

"But how will I survive as vibration?" You might as well ask, "How is consciousness possible at all?" There's no difference in the thing itself, intrinsically free of dense OM both before and after death. Spirit is none other than consciousness, in whatever circumstance, and thanks to its famed refusal of containment, we don't even need independent confirmation from departed spirits themselves, though we also possess this in abundance.

"But how will I—"

Shhh, let me tell you a secret: You are already in the afterlife. As the old saying goes, "We are just as much spirit now as we ever shall be."

Appendix J

Taking Ubiquity Literally:
What if They are not "from" anywhere and are not even "They"?

To see a World in a Grain of Sand
And a Heaven in a Wild Flower
Hold Infinity in the palm of your hand
And Eternity in an hour…
—William Blake

Ataguchu, tired due to cosmic loneliness, created others for company…
—Inca creation myth

During a podcast, I talked about remote viewing, a psychic ability that remains officially unexplained even fifty years after its conclusive demonstration at Stanford University.[1] An especially talented practitioner can sit in a room in Vermont, say, and "target" an office in China with her mind's eye—even focusing on one book and accurately drawing the characters on the spine. How is such a thing possible? It's possible because the term *remote viewing* turns out to be false.

I said, "There's nothing remote about it. Contrary to popular belief, it's not a matter of the viewer's consciousness actually *traveling* to China. Instead, she's accessing information that's available everywhere." It was a video podcast, so to emphasize my point, I drew a small circle in the air about ten inches from my nose. "That office in China? It's actually right *here*. All of its information, if you can tune in to it." I drew another circle. "And *here*, too."

I surprised my host with such a confident assertion; I'd never put it, even to myself, quite so bluntly. After the episode, I had to wonder not Is this true? but *How* is this true? How can we take ubiquity literally?

Could it be that the fundamental consciousness field is a *fractal*?

A fractal is a never-ending, infinitely complex pattern that is self-similar across different scales. It is created by repeating a simple process over and over in an ongoing feedback loop.[2]

It's an attractive analogy for sure, and it has the advantage of being a basic feature of the natural world, but it doesn't fill the bill because while all the manifestations of a fractal are self-similar, they are not self-*identical*; their varying size and shape means they couldn't replicate subtle source information—such as a Chinese character—because their size and shape *is* their information and therefore don't allow for finer details. Also, as fractals continue to form, they create an overall shape that is not symmetrical, not the same everywhere, its contents not uniformly distributed, whereas what we're looking for is a process that produces exactly the same information at every point.

The next candidate is the *hologram*. In its favor is that it relies on electromagnetic energy, which can perhaps stand for a corresponding IM (dark matter) energy that animates the fundamental consciousness field. In its familiar context, a hologram entails a beam of light passing through an object, which then scatters light onto a recording medium (such as film).

For us, the relevant quality is that every part of a hologram contains the whole, hence the Greek prefix *holo*; and *gramma* means "message."

> Holograms are like looking through a metal-mesh window-screen. Each little square contains an entire image, but an image seen from a slightly different viewpoint. Now pull your face away from the "screen door," and all the little squares combine to form the same scene.[4]

The only problem is that the more you subdivide the original image, the lower the resolution of each part, an informational loss ill suited to the remote viewing process.

We might imagine some alternative version of the holographic principle at work within the IM context that can avoid the same informational degradation. What if the data contained in that Chinese office—and in every other location—is shot through with enough IM energy and so efficiently as to create, by a process akin to diffraction, faithful reflections against some sort of recording medium that manifests before my nose and every other possible nose; after all, aren't the Akashic Records (by whatever name) supposed to store all information? This could be our holographic "film."

But think about it: We can't be talking about a *literal* hologram here—a single light source casting an image against a single backdrop—because our world, let alone the universe at large, is infinitely more complex than this. So, it would have to be a very different type of hologram wherein each and every data point serves as the original "whole" through which energy passes, creating an essentially infinite number of replica images distributed throughout space—anywhere a remote viewer may happen to sit and attempt to target this continent, this country, this province, this city, this office, this book. And wherever this remote viewer sits would need, as well, to contain available images of *all other data potentially sought*. This seems an absurdly contrived picture.

All of which, of course, is to say nothing about other, equally rich forms of information—emotions and thoughts, sounds and sensations—that cannot be categorized as visual representations but are easily picked up by genuine psychic mediums.

No, both the fractal and the hologram models are mere metaphors, and even as such they fall far short.

To cover the entire landscape of informational ubiquity, there is one known, non-metaphorical concept that fits. In physics and geometry, *isotropy* (from Greek *isos* "equal" and *trópos* "turn, way") means uniformity in all directions and orientations. Whatever else it is, the system that distributes information must be isotropic. What behaves this way in nature?

It all comes back to frequency and its information-carrying capacity; see Appendix I. But just as each radio station requires its own dedicated frequency, wouldn't each independent packet of information need this also? How can so many frequencies exist?

Well, it has surprised me to learn that within our familiar energy context, the resources are boundless.

> The electromagnetic spectrum is continuous and thus between any two frequencies there are an uncountable infinity of possible frequencies (just as there are uncountable numbers between 1 and 2). If you're prepared to go on dividing the spectrum up into small enough chunks, then there is literally no end to how many frequencies there are.[5]

For practical purposes, we chop this spectrum up arbitrarily to make it grok with our instruments, the only limiting factor being their range and subtlety.

Now, when it comes to the different form of energy wielded by the fundamental consciousness field (see Appendix C), we can presume that it, too, operates along a spectrum of frequencies and—because this is how spectrums are—that it is continuous. Moreover, although it can overlap with our electromagnetic spectrum—as when spirits affect electronics or materialize visibly—it stretches immeasurably higher, and the higher it is, the more information can be packed into each frequency; see Appendix I.

Finally, whereas the electromagnetic spectrum and the machines designed to receive and process it *are two distinctly different orders of thing*, requiring to be technologically bridged by receivers, no such gulf exists between the fundamental consciousness field at large and the mind of any given remote viewer or psychic medium, or your mind or mine. The two are one, sharing the same essence, the same origin, meaning that an individual consciousness is free to tune in directly, without mediation, to *any* of the limitless frequencies making up the fundamental consciousness field—the field that "knows" all information.

But how to locate the precisely right frequency—such as the one corresponding to a book title on a shelf seven thousand miles away—among infinite possibilities? As we saw in section 3.5, it's not a matter of searching and finding but rather of attunement, of tapping into a system already prepared for any question; the researchers at the SRI discovered that their best remote viewers could access their targets with nothing more to go on than the word "target." This uncanny efficiency speaks to the self-sufficient nature of the process. It's just like ordinary thinking as we experience it all the time; we don't oversee the journey before embarking on a train of thought—the train runs by itself. Yes, sometimes we *try* to remember something, but even then we're not in charge; we're only telling ourselves "target" and hoping for the best.

So, how does all this relate to UAPs and their occupants? It further reinforces the conclusion that the fundamental consciousness field operates autonomously, independent of flesh and blood (see Appendix K), and that frequency is the ultimate currency of information.

Evidently, though they can drop into our familiar reality frame, the visitors' natural frequency range is too high for them to linger long. During visitations, it does overlap with ours both physically and psychically, but most of the time they're out of frame. Where do they go?

Some claim they reside in vast subterranean cities or bases. I doubt that. They are seen descending into and rising from lakes and oceans and even passing through solid ground, but I think that given their low density, traveling down deep is essentially the same as streaking across our skies; neither offers a good clue as to any would-be headquarters.

What if, between appearances, they simply recede, dissolving back into a shared state of abiding rarefaction, like invisible vapor before the next rain? What if "visitors" plural is not even the right idea? What if at bottom it is, and always has been, a single autonomous consciousness—from nowhere and everywhere—seeking a home, a ground, identity, solidity, seeking concrete forms to inhabit, perpetually producing a kaleidoscopic menagerie of avatars on Laboratory Earth?

But the "alien races" seem so diverse, judging by reports, with competing agendas and sometimes even seen battling one another. Well, how better for an opportunistic spirit to generate interesting drama than through differentiation, through characters in conflict?

It is isotropic, this latent presence, manifesting wherever and whenever it pleases, hence the startling success of the CE5 movement; see the documentary "Contact: The CE5 Experience." Its true condition, like ours, is consciousness, but its IM/OM ratio is much higher, and, unlike us, it lacks its own assigned form of physical embodiment; instead, it has had to improvise, shapeshifting, fashioning a pantheon of incarnations that we see embedded in worldwide human mythologies.

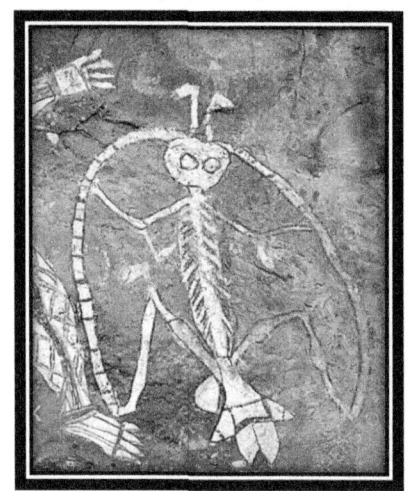

Namarrkon, the Lightning Man, 20,000 years old, one of the supernatural ancestors depicted at the aboriginal rock art site at Nourlangie Rock, Kakadu National Park, Australia; representations of "ant people" are common throughout the ancient world. Below: a ceramic vessel from Nazca, Peru, dated between 100 BC and 600 AD.

I'm guessing that when it began fiddling with life on our planet, however long ago, it worked with the raw genetic materials available at the time. That its appearance is typically described as insectile or reptilian may serve as a window into its earliest experiments, a broad timestamp. Insects and reptiles are the two most successful animal lines; still today, excluding microbes, one out of every four individuals on Earth is an ant. They arose here 400 million and 320 million years ago respectively, providing the predominant genetic ingredients long before mammals came on the scene; the "aliens" don't look like mammals, except for one much younger group—primates. Their resemblance to *Homo sapiens* and other hominids seems to represent a fresh wave of recombination with those first primordial genomes.

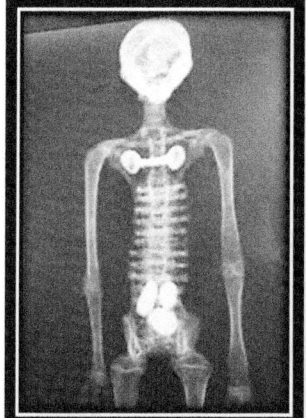

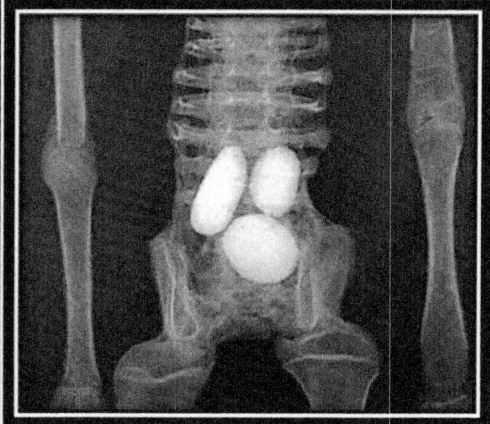

Egg-bearing reptilian humanoid mummy, discovered 2017, Nazca, Peru; C-14 dating places this hybrid specimen, one of many recently unearthed, at circa 1200 years old.

How does a disembodied consciousness accomplish such intricate biological wizardry? First, like every agent, it is part and parcel of the fundamental consciousness field, so it finds all frequencies available. Second, it has had untold millions of years to tune in to the necessary information, to learn, to practice, to translate knowing into action. Third, what is action but our old friend macro-PK, whose influence on the physical world we've tracked throughout the book? The force behind this zoological long game is no different.

And what of those fantastic flying machines? Same answer. If the actor in question can engineer DNA, hacking species, *hijacking life itself*, then surely it can extract metals and mold them into simple shapes—UAP apports in all their myriad permutations.

References

1. See Harold E. Puthoff and Russell Targ, *Mind-Reach: Scientists Look at Psychic Abilities*, Hampton Roads Publishing, Newburyport, MA: 2005 and Annie Jacobsen, *Phenomena: The Secret History of the U.S. Government's Investigations*

into Extrasensory Perception and Psychokinesis, Little, Brown and Company, New York: 2017.
2. fractalfoundation.org
3. From a group called Quantum Physics posting on Quora.com
4. William J. Beaty, University of Washington
5. physics.stackexchange.com

Appendix K
The Brain as Filter

Looking for consciousness in the brain is like looking inside a radio for the announcer.
—Nassim Haramein

For centuries, neurologists and psychic/spiritual researchers have been at odds over the nature of consciousness, the former insisting that it is produced by the brain alone, the latter that the brain serves merely as a receiver. For those looking on from the sidelines, these countervailing claims have seemed not only irreconcilable as they stand but also inherently unprovable—each hermetically sealed within its own ideological fortress. The situation is like the famous gestalt image that forces the eye to see either a vase or two faces, but never both at once.

Oh, neurologists think it's easy to prove their case: Simply damage or remove a portion of the brain and note the immediate impairment of consciousness. Of course, the other team replies, "You can take a hammer to a computer, too, but that doesn't mean you're ruining the Internet itself." The enduring question has been, How to design an experiment subtle enough to tease apart and test the two explanations, finally getting down to brass tacks.

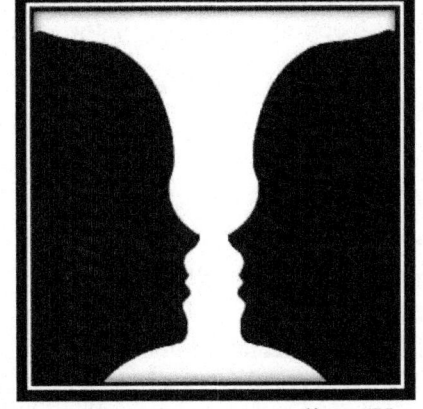

The advent of brain-imaging technology (fMRI) in 1990 seemed to promise just such a granular methodology. Unfortunately, watching brain regions "light up" differentially from conscious state to conscious state only demonstrates correlation, not causation—not ultimate source of thought.

Surprisingly, now, progress may be at hand through the very method long dismissed as pointless: inflicting brain damage. This kind of damage is only temporary, highly targeted by means of rTMS, Repetitive Transcranial Magnetic Stimulation.

In a study to appear in the journal *Cortex*, researchers present an experiment designed around the premise that the brain not only receives conscious information from beyond itself but also *filters out* much of it. The authors of "Enhanced Mind-Matter Interactions Following rTMS-Induced Frontal Lobe Inhibition" suggest a strong evolutionary advantage in curtailing psychic/spiritual (psi) influence on the daily lives of our species.

> The benefits of inhibiting psi might include preventing exposure to constant bombardment with irrelevant stimuli from telepathy, precognition, and clairvoyance that might divert attention away from environmental events threatening survival. The same notion might also apply to inhibiting mind-matter interactions that could cause chaos in the environment.[1]

The type of matter-mind interaction they assessed was the subjects' ability, both before and after the procedure, to cause micro-PK effects on a random event generator (REG), as described in section 3.6. The procedure was a "theta burst stimulation" (TBS) to the left medial middle frontal brain region, which "reduces cortical excitability for 20 to 30 minutes." Cortical excitability means the strength of neurons' response to stimulation; a TBS quiets this responsiveness in a location technically known as a "virtual lesion."

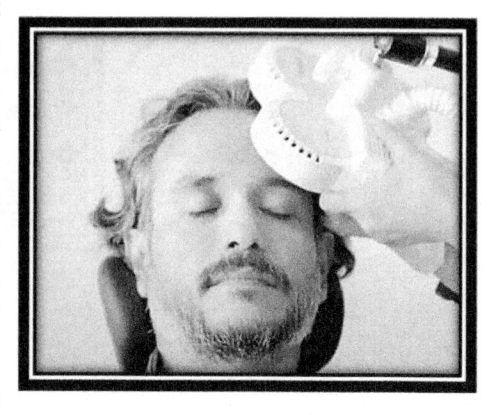

The researchers found that subjects' ability to accomplish micro-PK on the REG increased significantly immediately after the procedure.

> As predicted by our hypothesis, we demonstrated that healthy participants with reversible rTMS-induced lesions targeting the left medial middle frontal brain region showed larger right intention effects [ability to move a screen icon to the right through intention, a result that reflects success in affecting the REG] on a mind-matter interaction task compared to healthy participants without rTMS-induced lesions.[2]

Granted, this finding is an extremely small and preliminary step forward in substantiating the filter hypothesis; the authors concede as much while proposing that "studying participants with neurological [permanent] or reversible frontal lesions may facilitate detection and replication of psi effects in well-controlled studies." They also point toward the targeted use of psychedelics such as psilocybin, which can cause a "reduction of cerebral blood flow in the medial prefrontal cortex."[3]

A *reduction* of blood flow? Yes, it has been found that psychedelic trips involving an expansion of consciousness do not correlate to an explosion of brain activity. "Although the prevailing view has been that hallucinogens work by activating the brain," write Adam Halberstadt and Mark Geyer in *Scientific American*, "the results of a recent imaging study are challenging these conventional explanations."

The English author Aldous Huxley believed that the brain acts as a "reducing valve" that constrains conscious awareness, with mescaline and other hallucinogens inducing psychedelic effects by inhibiting this filtering mechanism. Even though Huxley proposed this idea in 1954, decades before the advent of modern brain science, it turns out that he may have been correct.[4]

Writing in *Nature*, Mo Costandi reports on a study published in the Proceedings of the National Academy of Sciences.[5]

> The researchers recruited 30 volunteers, all experienced users of hallucinogenic drugs, and scanned their brains twice: once after the participants had been given a salt-water placebo and once after the injection of a moderate dose of psilocybin, which produced a short "trip" that came on within seconds.

> "Psychedelics are thought of as 'mind-expanding' drugs, so it has commonly been assumed that they work by increasing brain activity," says David Nutt, a neuropsychopharmacologist at Imperial College London. "Surprisingly, we found that psilocybin actually caused activity to decrease in areas that have the densest connections with other areas." Furthermore, the intensity of the drug's effects [was associated] with the largest decreases.[6]

This same effect is seen, too, in the common phenomenon of "terminal lucidity," in which a person becomes suddenly fully present mentally, at the very end of life, after months or years of cognitive deterioration. Oddly, in such cases, the resurgence of consciousness does not occur progressively with the brain's slow decline; instead, it waits in the wings. Perhaps all of one's psychic energy is absorbed in the heavy lifting of the dying process until victory relieves the pressure, granting a final curtain call.

Deep meditation and time spent in sensory deprivation tanks also tend to suppress synaptic noise, clearing the way for altered states of consciousness and/or the release of latent psychic abilities. About the latter, see Jeff Tarrant's book *Becoming Psychic: Lessons from the Minds of Mediums, Healers, and Psychics* for further insights and experimental findings on the spiritually liberating effects of targeted Transcranial Magnetic Stimulation.

A radical limit case shows up in the recent annals of neurology. A certain type of "medical miracle" challenges the primacy of the brain itself, demonstrating that even under conditions of near-total deficit, consciousness can find a way.

> First described in *The Lancet* in 2007, the case of the man who appears to be missing most of his brain has been puzzling scientists ever since. The French man was 44 years old at the time, and the researchers explained that he'd lived most of his life without realizing anything was wrong with him. He only went to the doctor complaining of mild weakness in his left leg, and brain scans revealed that his skull was mostly filled with fluid, leaving just a thin outer layer of actual brain tissue.

Doctors think the majority of the man's brain was slowly destroyed over the course of 30 years by the build-up of fluid, a condition known as hydrocephalus. He'd been diagnosed with it as an infant and treated with a stent, but it was removed when he was 14, and since then, the majority of his brain seems to have eroded.

But despite his minimal remaining brain tissue, the man wasn't mentally disabled. He was working as a civil servant. He was also married with two children and was relatively healthy. His case study challenges our understanding of consciousness.[7]

* * *

In 1977, John Lorber, the campus doctor at Sheffield University, was treating a student of mathematics for a minor ailment. The student was bright, an honors student with an IQ of 126. Dr. Lorber examined the boy's head by Cat-scan to discover that the student had virtually no brain. The normal brain consists of two hemispheres that fill the cranial cavity, some 4.5cm deep. This student had a layer of cerebral tissue less than 1mm deep covering the top of his spinal column. The student had a condition called hydrocephalus in which the cerebrospinal fluid (clear colourless fluid) becomes dammed up.[8]

Nor do these two examples stand alone. Dr. Lorber evaluated more than 600 cases of profound hydrocephaly and half of them had an IQ normal or above. Upon careful examination, he described some of the subjects as having "no detectable brains" whatsoever.

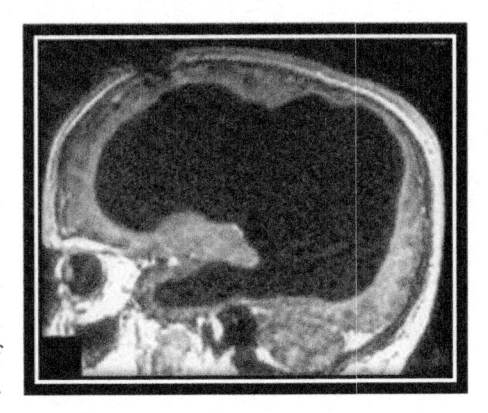

> Dr. Patrick Wall, professor of anatomy at University College, London, stated that there existed "scores" of accounts of people existing without discernable brains.

The importance of Lorber's work, Wall said, was that he had conducted a long series of systematic scanning, rather than simply collecting anecdotal material.

David Bower, professor of neurophysiology at Liverpool University, concluded that although Lorber's research did not indicate that the brain is unnecessary, it did demonstrate that [mental functions can occur] in conditions that conventional medical science would have thought impossible.[9]

References

1. Morris Freedman, Malcolm A. Binns, Jed A. Meltzer, Rohila Hashimi, Robert Chen, "Enhanced Mind-Matter Interactions Following rTMS-Induced Frontal Lobe Inhibition," *Cortex*, March 2024.
2. Ibid.
3. Ibid.
4. Adam Halberstadt and Mark Geyer, "Do Psychedelics Expand the Mind by Reducing Brain Activity?", *Scientific American* MAY 15, 2012
5. Robin L. Carhart-Harris, David Erritzoe, Tim Williams, David J. Nutt, "Neural correlates of the psychedelic state as determined by fMRI studies with psilocybin," *Proceedings of the National Academy of Science USA*, January 2012.
6. Mo Costandi, "Psychedelic chemical subdues brain activity," *Nature* (2012)
7. Fiona McDonald, "Science Alert," July 2016.
8. *The Irish Times*, November 2006.
9. Encyclopedia.com.

Appendix L
Suggested Experiments for Testing the MTR

As I described in section 4.9, the IM/OM synthesis is the foundational identity of matter as such. And since IM is not directly detectable by the instruments we currently possess, the relationship between the two matter types is inherently self-concealing. Lacking any means of teasing them apart for independent analysis, then, any experimental method will have to rely on an indirect or inferential approach in order to peek around the epistemological corner. Researchers will need to poke at reality in atypical ways so as to elicit measurable phenomena that are unexplainable within the OM context alone and instead call out the influence of another form of matter tightly fitting the description of IM in the MTR.

Unfortunately, most experimental trials designed along these lines will require the inclusion of an X factor—a psychically gifted participant. I say "unfortunately" only because of the fierce institutional and ideological resistance to such factors.

One of the few mainstream scientists curious and brave enough to investigate physical mediumship is Eckhart Kruse, specialist in robotics and computer vision and professor of Applied Computer Science at the Baden-Wurttemberg Cooperative State University in Germany.

The excellent video "Prof. Eckhard Kruse: Physical Mediumship - My perspective" on the Wendy Zammit channel takes us through his recent experiments with British medium Gary Mannion; especially pertinent for us is what's shown starting from the 31-minute mark. Mannion's wrists and ankles are firmly attached to the chair with cable ties, and motion sensors confirm that all four remain secure throughout his eventful trance sessions. Mannion sits inside a tall tent, a version of the traditional "cabinet" that mediums have used since the mid-1800s in order to focus their energy and shield themselves from the distractions of the séance room. With the medium in a trance state, we can see that the tent thrashes about wildly and even spins in full circles.

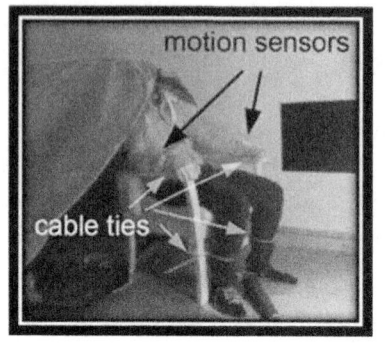

On June 20, 2023, I witnessed this same macro-PK outburst myself while attending one of Mannion's séances. It seemed as though the tent were caught up in a brief, localized hurricane, though the medium continued sitting calmly inside.

The entire tent contorts while the medium remains seated, wrists and ankles secured.

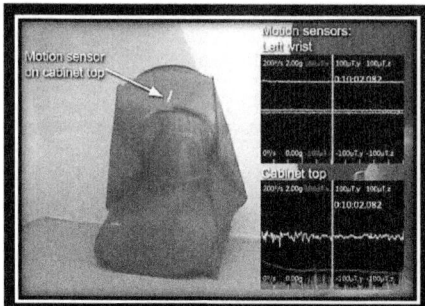

It blurs in the video because it is rotating so quickly.

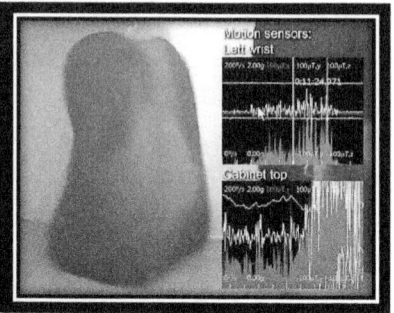

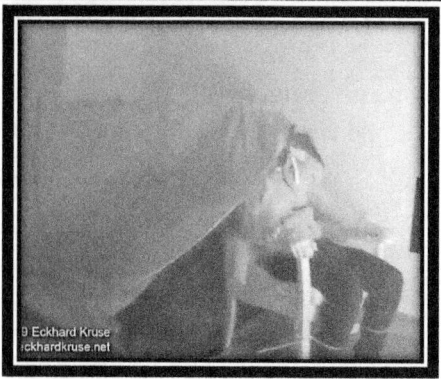

Eventually, the tent is yanked off entirely, revealing the medium still firmly restrained.

Of course, none of this by itself serves to validate the MTR theory. We need a sharper instrument. I share Dr. Kruse's remarkable evidence by way of example; it's not difficult to work with a physical medium, provided she or he is willing, or to obtain objective data through readily available technology.

Macro-PK in any form does, however, lay important groundwork in that the conventional OM-only paradigm stands abjectly mute in the face of such phenomena. What we need is an approach that uses macro-PK as a window into a sector of reality fitting the specific description of IM. None of these experiments, even if successful, will prove that so-called "dark matter," generally accepted by science, detected gravitationally on a galactic scale, is behind psychic/spiritual effects here on Earth. But they can indicate at least that *something closely akin to it*—an as-yet-undetermined type of matter of vanishingly minimal density—is crucially in play.

Experiment 1

- Replicate Crawford's scale experiments (section 4.3) with a physical medium test subject capable, at least sometimes, of increasing and decreasing the mass of an object at will.
- While she or he is affecting the object's mass, monitor the medium's weight as well.
- If during successful macro-PK attempts, the weight of object and medium are inversely proportional (as in the case of Kathleen Goligher), this will strongly suggest an exchange of matter types between the two, one type possessing a higher density, the other a lower.

Experiment 2

- Attach to or embed within the object to be levitated an array of highly sensitive thermometers in order to record any sudden temperature drop coinciding with success.

- If such a change is registered, this will corroborate a successful Experiment 1 by suggesting that the object's density is being altered, causing a temperature change.
- This experiment can be conducted with a group of subjects.

Experiment 3

- Attach to or embed within the object to be levitated an array of highly sensitive microphones in order to record any sounds of substrate displacement (as described in section 4.5) too subtle for the human ear.
- If such sounds coincide with levitation, this will agree with Dr. Colvin's analysis of "spirit raps" that, he found, "appear to involve the buildup of a stress *within a material*, culminating in an audible sound when the level of stress reaches a specific magnitude, and the stress is relieved."
- This experiment can be conducted with a group of subjects.

Experiment 4

- Use a small hyperbaric chamber, 100% airtight and designed to contain an elevated-pressure atmosphere. If the test subject can, repeatedly and through conscious intent, reduce the pressure inside the chamber, this will demonstrate that she or he (or they if a group) has (have) introduced a lower-pressure matter type into the sequestered atmosphere.
- If the lowest pressure achieved during this macro-PK period is lower than would be expected with the introduction of ordinary pressure at this altitude—that is, if it gets lower than room-pressure—this will conclusively demonstrate that the test subject has manipulated something other than ordinary air. The lower the minimum pressure achieved, the less satisfactorily will an OM-only paradigm account or it.

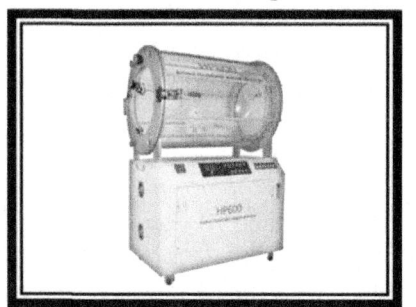

- This experiment can be conducted with a group of subjects.

Experiment 5

- As in Experiment 4, barometric pressure will be measured, this time inside a house with a history of apparent spirit presence.
- Set up barometers and thermometers in all the rooms of the house. Researchers will take continuous barometric pressure and temperature readings. If the pressure in one part of the house abruptly drops, the rest of the house remaining unchanged, this will be an affect unaccountable by "natural causes" conventionally understood, pointing to the influence of the sort of low-density IM/OM ratio proposed by the MTR.
- If at the same time and in the same room as the barometric pressure drop we also see a temperature drop, the rest of the house remaining unchanged, this will serve as reinforcement for the MTR interpretation.
- Such a result will also demonstrate that extremely localized air pressure and temperature drops can be sustained without being immediately dissipated into the higher ambient pressure of the rest of the house.

Christopher Noël holds a master's degree in Philosophy from Yale University. He has written extensively on the Sasquatch species and on psychic/spiritual phenomena. He lives in northern Vermont. www.TheNearnessofYou.net

Printed in Great Britain
by Amazon